PSYCHOLOGY

the basic principles

PSYCHOLOGY
the basic principles

by

JOHN F. HAHN

Professor of Psychology
University of Virginia

and

SANFORD LOPATER

Assistant Professor of Psychology
Christopher Newport College

1977

LITTLEFIELD, ADAMS & CO.
TOTOWA, NEW JERSEY

Published 1977 by
LITTLEFIELD, ADAMS & CO.
by special arrangement with Copeland & Lamm, Inc.

Copyright © 1977 by Copeland & Lamm, Inc.

Based upon *An Introduction to Psychology*
by John F. Hahn, copyright © 1962 by Copeland & Lamm, Inc.

Library of Congress Cataloging in Publication Data

Hahn, John F., and Sanford Lopater
    Psychology: The Basic Principles

    (A Littlefield, Adams Quality Paperback No. 324)
    Includes index.
        1. Psychology.   I.   Lopater, Sanford, joint author.
II.   Title.
[DNLM: 1. Psychology.   BF121 H148p]
BF131.H153   150   76-55786
ISBN O-8226-0324-1

Printed in the United States of America

Preface

This book aims to present a concise survey of the basic principles of psychology. Concrete examples have been used throughout to illustrate the concepts, theories, and experiments discussed; and often there is an indication, either explicit or implicit, of the kind of evidence upon which a conclusion is based. As the book is compactly written, we suggest that it not be read too swiftly. The reader is encouraged to devise his own examples in order to enhance the personal relevance of the material and thereby gain greater mastery of it. The reader should also understand that the information that follows is constantly being tested and refined in order to determine the most appropriate application of reliable facts.

Students in first-year psychology courses will find it a good plan to correlate topics in this book with topics in the course as it progresses, and to remember that introductory psychology courses differ in the emphasis they give to different topics. Those who use this book as a course-review aid should keep in mind the fact that different instructors organize their courses differently.

This book has not been written for students only, however. We would like to think that this survey of basic principles will prove interesting and informative to others as well, among them those who are somewhat skeptical about psychology to begin with. Whatever the reader's special interests, whatever his occu-

pation, whatever his goals, an understanding of the basic principles of psychology will prove rewarding, enriching, stimulating,
and very possibly useful.

In writing this book we followed the general plan of a book
called *An Introduction to Psychology* written some years ago
by John F. Hahn, who wishes to acknowledge gratefully that
the major burden of writing the present book fell upon Sanford
Lopater, and to say that this book is the better for it. We
are also grateful to Sylvia Caldwell, whose conscientious and
meticulous typing of the preliminary and final drafts of the
manuscript is very much appreciated. Our thanks, too, to Law-
rence W. Lamm and Patricia White for their encouragement
and valuable editorial recommendations.

J. F. H.
S. L.

Contents

PSYCHOLOGY

the basic principles

Chapter 1

Introduction

The word *psychology* and especially the adjective *psychological* in everyday usage refer to aspects of an individual's "state of mind" or to an individual's interpretation of someone else's state of mind. The bodily mechanisms and processes involved would belong to the field of *physiology*. In this way psychological and physiological approaches are contrasted in their dealing with the same problem.

However, in developing psychology as a science, it has been found that scientific method can be applied most successfully by laboratory study to the full extent that this is feasible. And in laboratory experiments not only can behavior itself be studied, but so can its physiological and biological bases, with reactions recorded and results interpreted in psychological terms. Such experimentation is performed mainly with the use of animals as subjects. Conclusions can be drawn as to appropriate interpretation of these experiments in the study of human behavior. As we will see, certain human activities cannot be studied through laboratory experimentation. Thus our presentation will adapt itself to the practical scientific possibilities in each area of behavior.

Psychology is quite diversified. At first you may be surprised at the variety of topics covered in the following chapters, but psychologists are interested in everything that affects human and animal behavior. Whether it be heredity or upbringing, whether it be social pressures or learning, whether it be how the senses process incoming information or how the body reacts to stress, if it affects behavior, psychologists want to understand it.

Psychologists are not the only students of behavior, of course. Artists, theologians, authors, poets, playwrights, and philosophers, to name only a few, have long dealt extensively and effectively with most of the topics in the following chapters, and have provided many valuable insights. Yet concern with understanding and prediction of behavior lies especially in the domain of the psychologist.

The information presented in this book is not directed solely toward a description of the nature of human and animal behavior. Rather, it is an attempt to systematize facts, describe them carefully, and suggest lawful relationships among them. In addition, unanswered questions are presented throughout the following chapters in an attempt to point out where further facts are needed. Various fact-finding techniques specific to the different subdisciplines in psychology are also noted. The value of observational, experimental, and clinical methods will become apparent in connection with a diversity of research problems.

A number of perspectives are useful in the study of human and animal behavior. An understanding of the biological functions of organisms is one example. Knowledge concerning the ways in which people and animals receive information through their sense organs about their environment, and the ways in which the brain acts on this information, are implicit in this approach. Another perspective involves behavior in social settings. Here the major concern is with interactions among those in groups of various kinds, for example the family or the occupational setting. Still another perspective involves cognitive processes such as learning, memory, and thought. And there is the area of personality. These are but a few of the viewpoints that may be used in observing and interpreting behavior. Strict adherence to only one perspective results in limited understanding of behavior dynamics and therefore necessarily limited applications of information to real-life problems. While such an eclectic approach may seem like a tall order to the beginning student in psychology, it is a goal worthy of earnest effort.

In studying the various subdisciplines of psychology, the student will note, as mentioned above, that both laboratory and naturalistic observation techniques are employed. Certain problems are explored in the controlled setting of the laboratory, where stimuli and responses may be precisely determined. Other problems can only be explored in the real-life setting in which they occur. Neither method is inherently superior to the other, as each works best for different problems. The behavioral scientist thus has at his disposal a variety of fact-finding methods, each appropriate for a specific type of problem, each with its own strong points.

Psychologists use humans and a variety of subhumans in their laboratory and observational investigations. It is difficult and sometimes risky to make generalizations about human behavior on the basis of subhuman studies, and for this reason psychologists are cautious in applying such data to humans. However, for reasons of convenience and ethics many preliminary investigations employ subhumans. Where physiological manipulations are required, where the rapid breeding of successive generations of animals is called for, where close and total control of the environment is necessary, and where an organism's behavioral history must be thoroughly known, experimental and observational investigations profit from the employment of subhuman species.

So much for your introduction to Psychology. Let's begin.

Chapter 2

Behavior and Heredity: Physiological Psychology

All behavior is basically a reflection of both our genetic inheritance and the functioning of the nervous system. The means by which temperamental and physical attributes are inherited, the ways in which they interact with differing environments, and the expectancies we hold for their appearance are all issues of interest to psychologists. Also, the complexity of our behavior is a good indicator of the sophistication and capability of our nervous system. We will therefore examine the way in which the nervous system is built and a few characteristics of its function. Our understanding of behavior will be enhanced if we learn something about these topics.

THE GENETIC BASIS OF BEHAVIOR

To what extent is heredity involved in our psychological makeup? Can intelligence, temperament, or special talents be the result of our genetic inheritance? Heredity and the environment operate together. Their individual effects are difficult to separate; we can seldom determine the specific, proportionate effect of each. In eight generations of the Bach family, whose most famous member was Johann Sebastian, there were 99 males; of these, 50 were competent musicians, most of them being composers as well as performers. We cannot easily say whether this display of talent was the result of inheritance or of the fact that Bach children were brought up in musical surroundings. Psychologists are interested in both the genetic aspects of inheritance and the degree to which inherited characteristics are modified by the influence of the environment.

Genetic Mechanisms. When the genetic contributions of a male and female join, 23 *chromosomes* from each will combine. The cell from which the organism will develop has 46 chromosomes which will determine the physical and psychological makeup and potential of the offspring. These chromosomes are made up of many *genes*, tiny chemical packets that serve as a blueprint for all subsequent development of the body's several kinds of cells. These genes are arranged on chromosomes in a way similar to peas in a pod. When the male's sperm fertilizes the female's ovum (egg), genes from the father become paired with genes that serve similar functions from the mother. The development of the offspring is thus determined by the genetic contributions of its parents.

The influence of each gene in a gene pair is not equal; the appearance of gene-controlled characteristics can be determined by the dominant or recessive nature of the gene. If one gene of a pair is dominant and the other recessive, the characteristic produced by the dominant gene is the one that will appear, rather than the one that the recessive gene governs. Dominant gene effects interact with recessive gene effects. For example, a gene for brown eyes is dominant and a gene for blue eyes is recessive. If both genes in a pair are dominant, a person's eyes will be brown. If one gene is dominant and the other recessive, his eyes will be brown, but he can transmit to some of his offspring a recessive gene for blue eyes. If an individual happens to receive recessive genes from both parents, then his eyes will be blue, and he will transmit to his offspring only the recessive genes for blue eyes. However, any of these offspring who receive one dominant gene from the other parent will have brown eyes. Only a few traits in humans are governed by a single gene in this way. Certain taste sensitivities and some blood types are other examples. We now realize that many physical and most psychological traits are determined by more than one set of genes; these are called *polygenic* traits.

It can be seen that inheritance mechanisms are complicated. We seldom recognize the role of combinations of dominant and recessive genes in arriving at the idea of our own "individuality," yet our appearance and behavior reflect only one of a tremendous number of potential outcomes of our genetic makeup.

The Effect of Environment. A second area of interest to psychologists concerns the effect of the environment on genetically inherited characteristics. This can best be studied in species in which generations quickly succeed each other. Laboratory rats are an example. When some members of a given species are separated from other members of the same species and reproduce only among themselves, we call this a "strain" of animals. Such a strain is a genetically pure population of members of a species. It typically takes many generations of these matings to establish this purity. One good way to study the impact of the environment on physically or behaviorally transmitted characteristics is to expose two strains of laboratory animals to the same environment. If we observe measurably different types or amounts of specific behaviors in these two strains then we can say that these differences are due to the genetic makeup of these animals, not their environment. Strains of laboratory rats have been shown to differ significantly in their aggressiveness, sexual behavior, and learning facility.

Even though physical or behavioral characteristics are genetically determined, they may be altered by environmental action. For example, it is thought that some forms of heart disease are inherited. However, by altering dietary, smoking, and exercise habits an individual may escape the effects of this disease. This type of information takes a long time to accumulate and verify. Measuring the impact of environments on people is difficult as there are few counterparts in the human population to pure strains of laboratory animals. There is evidence that environmental factors have a great effect on such aspects of the personality as emotionality and assertiveness, a comparatively small effect on attributes that come under the heading of "intelligence," and even somewhat of an effect on the sensitivity of the sense organs. Much of the information bearing on the question of environmental influence has to do with maturation.

Maturation. Maturation may be thought of as both a behavioral process and a process of physical growth and development. The term includes such concepts as neurological growth and refinement, progressive improvement of such skills as walking and talking, and the appearance of qualitatively different forms of behavior as individuals grow to adulthood. It implies progressive, orderly biological development. The extent to which behavioral capabilities are the result of genetically determined characteristics or environmental influences is an issue of long-standing interest in psychology. As an example, note that infant salamanders fresh from their eggs do not swim. The ability to swim appears several days after the first movements are made. Is maturation or practice responsible for this behavior? Their swimming ability does not result from practice, for if sala-manders are anesthetized before any movements appear and are removed from the anesthetic at the normal age for swimming, they swim, although they have had no opportunity for practice. A separate experiment shows that the anesthetic itself has no side effects which influence the outcome.

Two types of experiments have been used to determine the respective roles of heredity and environment in the maturation of behavior. In one, subjects with the same or similar heredity are observed in situations in which there are differences in the amount of time or practice they have. In the other, subjects have different heredity but the same or similar amounts of time or practice in various situations.

Studies with Practice as a Variable. The following four ex-amples will illustrate the manner in which different amounts of practice in a situation have been investigated in trying to determine the role of heredity and environment in maturation, when heredity is the same or similar.

HOPI INDIAN INFANTS. The age at which Hopi infants first walked after they had been cradled in the orthodox Hopi fashion was compared to the age of first walking of Hopi infants who had been cradled in the conventional American fashion. In the former method, for the first three months after birth the infants were bundled in cloth bands and tied to a cradle board to be worn by the mother on her back. Very little activity was pos-sible. They were free of this restriction for only about an hour a day. It had been suggested that such a lack of opportunity for practice in locomotion would have the effect of delaying the time at which the infant would begin such practice and thereby delay the time at which the infant eventually walked.

There was no significant difference in the average age at which the two groups of infants first walked, whichever way they had been cradled. Lack of practice did not delay the development of this skill; age of first walking was determined by maturation independent of experience.

IDENTICAL TWINS. There are two different kinds of twins:

fraternal and identical. Fraternal twins, also called *dizygotic*, are the result of two eggs being fertilized by two sperm; they are as genetically similar to one another as siblings. Identical twins, also called *monozygotic*, are the result of one egg being fertilized by one sperm and then splitting in two shortly after fertilization; they are genetically identical.

A pair of identical twins was selected for study. Neither of these twins climbed stairs at the age of forty-six weeks. Then for six weeks, one of the twins was given ten minutes of daily practice in stair-climbing; at the end of this training period she climbed stairs readily. She then stopped practice, and after a week the other twin started practicing. After two weeks of practice, the second twin climbed stairs as well as the first had after six weeks of practice. One week later, during which neither twin had practice, both were still equally proficient.

These results indicate that the first twin took three times as long in her training because she had started earlier in her maturational development. This example raises the important issue of *maturational readiness.* Any systematic training prior to the nervous system's development to a certain point will bring about only temporary improvement or no improvement, at the cost of much longer, and often frustrating, training.

In reference to the distinction made above between dizygotic and monozygotic twins, it is important and interesting to note that heritability may be instrumental in the appearance of certain traits in both members of monozygotic twins more often than in dizygotic twins. Some of these traits include schizophrenia, manic-depressive psychosis, male homosexuality, and alcoholism. Also, studies have been made of monozygotic twins that have been reared apart. The results indicated strikingly similar performance on intelligence tests.

INFANT CHIMPANZEES AND CATS.   Shortly after birth, three infant chimpanzees were moved to surroundings which severely restricted the visual stimulation they received as they grew up. Two of them were reared in darkness. One was reared in a large plastic dome which admitted diffused light but made it impossible to see forms and shapes outside. After a little over half a year, the chimpanzees were moved back to their regular quarters in the animal park.

In the two animals reared in the dark, degeneration had taken place in some of the cells of the retina of the eye. This degeneration did not occur in the chimpanzee who had been reared in the diffused light.

All three animals were impaired in their ability to discriminate visual stimuli such as shapes and faces. A week of training was required before the chimpanzee reared in diffused light learned to recognize a large yellow disc with black stripes, though a normally reared chimpanzee can do so immediately. All three animals eventually appeared to develop normal vision after they had been returned to a normal visual environment.

Another investigation, involving kittens, has shown that environmental stimulation is important in the development of normal visual abilities. The part of the brain that processes visual information functions in the same way in kittens and adult cats. If a kitten has one eye sewn shut before its eyes normally open, and the eye remains closed until the kitten is a few months old, the vision in that eye will be significantly impaired thereafter. Also, nerve cells in the visual part of the brain will not respond appropriately to patterned stimuli presented to the eye that had been closed.

IMPRINTING. Newly hatched ducklings or goslings will follow almost any moving object which they see within a few hours after hatching. This object is usually their mother. It is thought that imprinting is a particularly important aspect of social development in these animals. Once the imprinting has taken place it is very difficult to break the bond which has been established. Imprinting will take place at a certain critical, optimum time after hatching. When imprinting does not take place in this "critical period" it is somewhat weaker; the attachment is not as strong. This is an example in which the environmental influence must be properly timed with respect to the development of the organism.

Studies with Heredity as a Variable. Another type of experiment has been carried out in which subjects with different heredity have been observed in similar situations. A few examples will clarify this case.

CHIMPANZEE AND MAN. A seven-month old female chimpanzee called Gua and a nine-month old baby boy, Donald, were raised as brother and sister, and the attempt was made to treat them as similarly as possible. The chimpanzee was earlier in developing such skills as walking, using a spoon, and obeying verbal instructions. Nine months later the boy had caught up in these skills, and was also developing capacities, such as language, which the chimpanzee was not.

INTELLECTUAL DEFICITS.   A few types of intellectual deficit are known to be of genetic origin. Special education and practice are of some help in these cases, but these environmental influences are of much less significance in determining the intelligence of these individuals than are genetic factors.

Conclusions about Practice and Heredity.   To sum up, maturation limits (1) the highest rate of development, (2) the highest final level of development, (3) the optimal time of practice or environmental effects, (4) the variety of behaviors in an organism's repertoire.

Other Studies of Maturation.   One area of study of particular interest to developmental psychologists has concerned the determination of the ages at which babies and young children commonly develop various skills such as creeping, grasping, walking, and so on. An assortment of techniques has been used to collect this information. One such method involves simple, standardized observational procedures involving the infant or child in uncontrolled, natural surroundings. A second method concerns clinical settings in which observational techniques are coupled with an interview format involving an exchange of information between an observer and subject. A third method involves experimentation in the laboratory setting where stimuli and responses may be accurately measured, controlled, and categorized. Drawbacks of the artificial environment of the laboratory seem to trade off with the advantages of precise, measurable documentation of experimental manipulations. A combination of these procedures may be employed in the investigation of diverse aspects of heredity-environment interaction. A few generalizations have emerged from the application of these techniques to various aspects of the study of maturation in infants and children.

NORMAL VARIABILITY.   There are considerable normal differences between one child and another in the ages at which maturational readiness for a particular skill appears. One child may be ready for walking or toilet training at less than half the age of another.

DIRECTION OF DEVELOPMENT.   Although different children may mature at markedly different rates, the order in which skills develop is quite similar from one child to the next. The general principle governing this sequence is that the direction of development is *cephalo-caudal* (head to tail) and *proximo-distal* (trunk to extremities). For example, the infant can raise his head before he can raise his hips, and can reach before he can grasp an object.

Instincts. Whenever we observe seemingly automatic, stereotyped behavior in ourselves, behavior that we don't take time to think about, we are likely to call it instinctive. In actuality, few if any human behaviors can really be called instinctive. The term *instinct* has a fairly strict definition. It refers to a rather permanent pattern of behavior that is always elicited in the same form by the same stimulus or pattern of stimuli and is specific to one species. It is interesting to observe the honeybee locate honey and easily find its way back to its hive. At first we might say that the honeybee is "intelligent." But we are actually observing instinctive behavior; all members of that species of honeybee will do the same thing in response to a certain cluster of environmental stimuli. We cannot say that the honeybee is "thinking." Other animal behaviors that are instinctive include the migration of certain species of birds and fish, species-specific bird songs, and the means by which certain fish and mammals claim and protect a territory for their own. Again we observe the relationship between innate, genetically "wired in" patterns of behavior and the environmental stimuli that are necessary to elicit them.

One area of biology is concerned with such instinctive and species-specific behaviors and deals primarily with comparing behavior in several species observed in natural settings. This is called *ethology*. The ethologist studies sensory capacities, food location and retrieval habits, fixed patterns of behavior that are elicited by unique stimuli, migration, hibernation, the concept of territoriality, and many other topics with regard to diverse species. More of a biological than psychological point of view is employed, and the methods and rationale of the ethologist are often useful in the study of human social behavior. This discipline deals with what is seemingly "automatic" and highly adaptive to a species of animal.

People commonly believe that they have instincts; it is doubtful that they do. Instincts here refer to fairly complex, ritualized sequences of behavior and do not include breathing, chewing, etc. Such behaviors as mothering, self-preservation, sexuality, and affiliation have been called "instinctive." Yet these are not permanent patterns of behavior; they are not observed in identical form in all people; they are not elicited by the same stimuli. The human does not really need instincts for his preservation. He does not need to rely on automatic, unthinking behavior patterns. Our cognitive capacities allow us to reason, remember, and communicate in flexible ways to meet the needs of diverse situations.

THE NERVOUS SYSTEM

The nervous system has increased in size and complexity in the course of evolution, yet the basic structural and functional principles are very similar throughout the animal kingdom. The diversity of behavior in a given species is a reflection of the activity and intricacy of this major body system.

Parts of the Nervous System. The nervous system is composed of specialized cells that receive, transmit, and select signals very rapidly. Its organization and functioning are very complex. Certain parts of the nervous system have their own restricted functions, while other parts are not restricted in function.

The Neuron. The neuron is a cell specialized for receiving, processing, and conducting brief, minute electrical charges called *action potentials.* Different parts of the nerve cell appear to be built specifically for each of the above functions (Figure 1). Fine, twig-like filaments carry information to the neuron's cell body; these are *dendrites.* The *cell body,* also called the *soma,* initiates and provides the energy for the action potential. Long extensions from the cell body carry information away from the nerve cell; these are *axons.* Axons may be relatively thick or thin, depending partly on whether they have a coating of a fatty substance called *myelin.* Axons may vary in length from a fraction of an inch to several feet; they range in diameter from 1/1000th of an inch to 1/50,000 of an inch. A *nerve* is a bundle of these axons. *Afferent* nerves carry information into the brain or spinal cord so that neurons there can process and interpret it. *Efferent* nerves carry action potentials away from the brain or spinal cord, to muscles for instance.

The Synapse. The synapse is a junction between one neuron and another; it is the point at which action potentials are transferred. Nerve cells do not really touch each other as synapses; there is actually a very narrow, fluid-filled gap, and certain chemicals convey the nerve impulse across it. There are literally billions of synapses in the nervous system, with some neurons

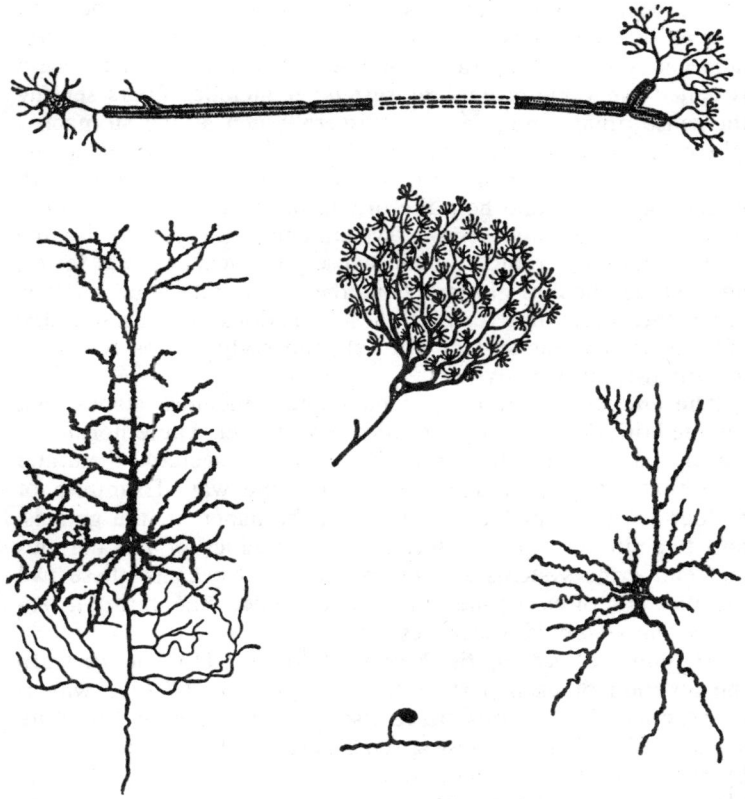

Fig. 1. Various Types of Neurons

each having up to 10,000. Synapses resemble multiple switches which permit any of a number of different routings of nerve impulses. In addition to synapses that transfer action potentials from one neuron to another, there are some that inhibit or block this transfer. Thus the number of action potentials coming from a neuron and the amounts of time between them reflect a complicated interplay between excitatory and inhibitory synapses.

Organization of the Nervous System. The *central nervous system* includes the brain and spinal cord and makes up most of the weight of the nervous system. The *peripheral nervous system* includes nerve fibers going to and from the central nervous system. One branch of the peripheral nervous system is called the *somatic nervous system*; it includes fibers serving the sense organs, muscles, and viscera (such as the stomach). The other branch of the peripheral nervous system is called the *autonomic nervous system*; it includes fibers that connect with endocrine glands and help the organism meet emergency situations. The autonomic nervous system can cause you to breathe deeper and more rapidly; it can cause your heart to beat faster, and redirect the flow of blood from the viscera into your muscles. After the threat that caused these reactions had passed, the autonomic nervous system can help the body organs return to a normal level of activity.

The *endocrine system*, just mentioned, includes glands that secrete hormones directly into the bloodstream. These hormones travel to an organ distant from the gland that secreted them and alter that "target" organ's activity in some way. Examples of endocrine glands include the thyroid, the pancreas, the gonads, and the pituitary gland. Because the activities of ·the nervous and endocrine systems are interrelated, and because these two systems are often connected to each other, the term *neuro-endocrine system* is sometimes used.

Methods of Studying the Nervous System. How do we learn the function of each part of the nervous system? One way is to examine the nervous tissue itself to see what its structure suggests. Another is to test specific parts of the nervous system by rendering them inoperative or by stimulating them. We can also measure the differences in electrical activity in various parts of the nervous system.

Neuroanatomy. The neuroanatomist studies the gross and microscopic structure of the nervous system. He is also interested in different ways of preparing nervous tissue for microscopic examination. He examines different types of neurons, nerve fiber pathways, and interconnections of cells in the nervous system. For example, neuroanatomists found that the retina, the mosaic of sensory cells at the back of the eye, is connected in an orderly, regular fashion to a part of the surface of the brain. When we look at a square, the image of that square on the retina results in a corresponding (though not exactly square) pattern of activity in that part of the brain. Thus the anatomist provides information which shows how structure is related to function.

Destruction.   One way to find out about the function of a part of the nervous system is to destroy it and note any changes in the organism's behavior. Although a cause-and-effect relationship may not always be clear, results are usually highly informative. We can learn about the function of the nervous system when destruction is the result of accidental trauma, disease, or deliberate experimental removal of tissue (*ablation*). Laboratory techniques have been used to destroy very small areas of the brain by using brief, minute amounts of electrical current to produce localized lesions. Such small lesions can have dramatic effects on behavior as we shall see later. It is the role of the neuroanatomist to verify the exact location of these lesions.

Stimulation.   Physiological psychologists commonly use surgical techniques to implant permanently tiny stimulating electrodes in certain areas of the brain. Upon recovery from the surgery, these areas are electrically stimulated and changes in the experimental animal's behavior are noted. (This electrical stimulation is not painful, nor is it strong enough to destroy brain tissue.)

The brain surfaces of conscious human patients undergoing brain surgery have sometimes been electrically stimulated. Since the brain itself is not sensitive to pain, only a local anesthetic is needed, and the patients remain fully conscious during the operation. The aim of the operations is the removal of diseased tissue from the brain. Before removing any, the surgeon needs to pinpoint the location of various brain areas, so he applies weak electric currents at various points on the surface of the brain. Stimulation at some points causes parts of the body to move; when other points are stimulated, the patients report various sensations and sometimes memories. Thus, as a by-product of the operations, information about the brain is gained which cannot be obtained from the study of animals.

Another way to stimulate the brain is to apply certain chemicals to its surface or to use narrow tubes to implant these chemicals in deeper brain structures. In this way something can be learned about the biochemistry of the functioning of certain brain areas, and the action of certain drugs can be assessed.

Recording Techniques. Electrical activity in different parts of the brain and nervous system can be recorded by placing pickup electrodes appropriately and amplifying the signals to record the ongoing electrical activity as well as changes in this activity in response to various environmental stimuli. Accurate stimulus-response relationships can thus be determined. The activity of larger or smaller brain areas can be recorded by using large or small pickup electrodes. The *electroencephalograph* (usually referred to as *EEG*) records the electrical activity of large areas of the human brain by means of several recording electrodes placed on the scalp. Techniques have also been developed by which the electrical activity in the nervous systems of anesthetized animals can be picked up with very small electrodes placed directly into the nervous system. Moreover, techniques are in use whereby activity in the brains of experimental animals can be recorded, amplified, and transmitted to a receiver so that records of brain activity may be obtained while the unanesthetized animal goes about its normal activities.

THE BRAIN AND BEHAVIOR

Is all of our brain involved in all of our behavior, or do certain parts of the brain serve certain behaviors? In other words, are behavioral functions localized in specific brain regions? To a major extent the answer to this question is "yes." For example, sensory, motor, emotional, and cognitive aspects of our behavior each have a reasonably specific, limited part of the brain devoted mainly to each type of activity. However, it is seldom that one part of the brain functions in isolation of other parts. A great deal of interaction usually occurs. One important area of human development involves an infant learning to interpret information coming in through one of the senses with the aid of information coming in through another. This is called *intermodal transfer*, and may be an example of the nervous system's early interaction activity. When an infant uses both vision and the sense of touch to learn that certain objects are "hard," the vision and touch areas of the brain are each functioning separately but they are interacting, too. Nerve fibers connecting these two areas of the brain may be helping this infant learn the meaning of "hard."

Another interesting point concerns the way that localized brain functions have changed in the course of evolution. The more sophisticated aspects of an animal's behavior are usually controlled by the more newly evolved brain structures. These are found in the most *rostral* (head) end of the brain, located above and in front of older subcortical areas. The process by which increasingly complex behavioral functions are controlled by progressively rostral brain structures is called *encephalization*. The most complex brain area, and the latest to evolve, is the cerebral cortex. A discussion of this structure begins a summary of our current understanding of brain function.

The Cerebral Cortex.   The cerebral cortex is composed of the brain's outermost nerve cell layers. It is commonly referred to as "grey matter." Various areas of the cortex are involved in specific behavioral functions; these areas have received much attention because they are so accessible. Figure 2 shows the parts of the cortex referred to below.

Visual Area.   This part of the brain is also called the *occipital cortex*. The spatial aspects of the world we see are spatially

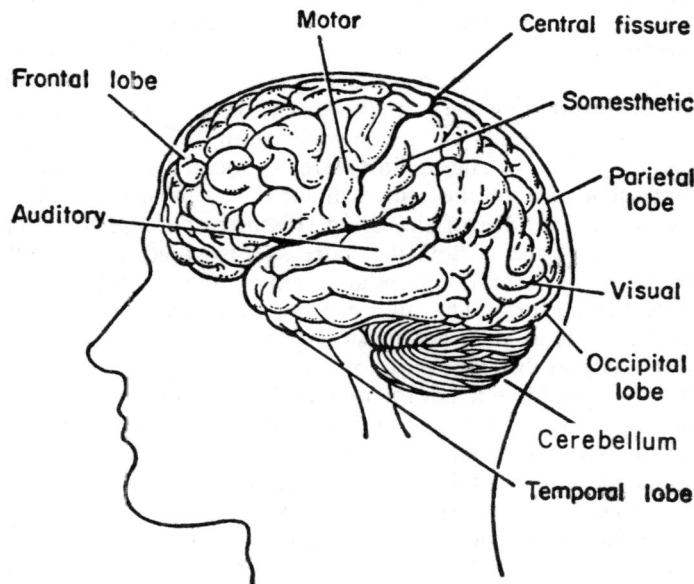

Fig. 2.   The Brain

represented on the cortex of the occipital lobe, where there is a distorted map of our visual world. The map's distortion consists in allotting proportionately more area to that part of the visual field which we look at directly than is allotted to the peripheral portions of the visual field. This map-like order is preserved throughout the visual pathway between the eye and the occipital cortex. Recently it has been discovered by using recording techniques that individual neurons in the occipital cortex are very sensitive and respond selectively to visual stimuli of diverse shape and orientation.

Destruction of part of the visual cortex results in blindness in the corresponding part of the visual field. Total destruction, due, for example, to disease or gunshot wound, results in total blindness in man. This is called *cortical blindness*, and its behavioral manifestations are quite different from those in which the eyes are nonfunctional. For example, the cortically blind individual may never learn to avoid obstacles by tapping a cane and listening to echoes, and exhibits an exceptionally poor capacity to remember the spatial characteristics of his surroundings, for example, the locations of pieces of furniture.

Electrical stimulation of the visual area in conscious human subjects undergoing surgery results in bright stars or pinwheels in the corresponding parts of the visual field. Complete visual images, such as faces or places, are not seen.

Auditory Area. The auditory area is located in the wall of the lateral fissure of the temporal lobe. (A *fissure* is a deep groove in the surface of the brain. Fissures increase the total surface area of the cortex; the more sophisticated an animal's behavioral repertoire, the more apparent is the wrinkled appearance of the cortex.) The auditory cortex is *tonotopically* arranged; sounds of different musical pitch cause maximal electrical activity in different parts of the auditory cortex.

Destruction of one temporal lobe has little effect upon hearing. Ablation experiments on laboratory animals indicate that even though it is tonotopically organized, the auditory cortex is not essential for simple pitch discrimination but it does have a role in the perception of melodies.

Electrical stimulation of the auditory cortex in conscious human subjects results in perceptions of buzzes and clicks. Stimulation does not yield reports of voices or of music.

In comparison to the visual area, the auditory cortex does

not have as large a spatial representation on the surface of the brain.

Somesthetic Area. The cortex on the posterior lip of the central fissure is a representation of the body surface. This "map" is also distorted. Larger areas of brain surface are devoted to those parts of the body where tactile sensitivity is greatest, such as the tongue, lips, hands, and genitals. The somesthetic cortex also monitors the position of our limbs in space, the degree to which our joints are bent, and the amount of tension on our muscles.

Destruction of the somesthetic cortex leads to a decrease in tactile sensitivity and may interfere with our ability to recognize objects by touch without the use of our eyes. This condition is known as *agnosia.*

Electrical stimulation in the somesthetic area of the conscious human patient yields reports of buzzing and tingling sensations felt in the part of the body corresponding to the cortical point stimulated.

Motor Area. On the strip of cortex along the front of the central fissure there is a motor map of the body. It, too, is a distorted map, proportionately more area being devoted to those body parts capable of more refined, nicely adjusted movements. The motor cortex serves as the "command post" from which instructions originate, telling the limbs whether or not to move, and if so, how much and how fast. The motor area is the beginning point of the nervous system's neatly arranged *descending pathways.* The term "efferent," defined earlier, refers to these pathways. Nerve fibers which originate in the motor area eventually influence muscles in the most peripheral parts of our extremities. These fibers course downward through the spinal cord and then outward to the limbs.

When parts of the motor area are damaged, either experimentally or through the effects of, for example, a stroke, paralysis may result in the corresponding part of the body. The degree of paralysis depends upon the amount and location of the damage. In some cases, this paralysis is not permanent and there may be some recovery of function.

Electrical stimulation in the motor area of a conscious human patient results in simple, sometimes spasmodic, movements of those parts of the body corresponding to the cortical points stimulated. Skilled, adjustive movements are not obtained.

The *cerebellum* is another part of the brain involved in motor behavior. It is discussed below under "Subcortical Structures."

Frontal Lobes. The functions of the frontal and prefrontal lobes are not completely understood. Some behaviors attributed to these areas include fine motor coordination, speech, intellectual ability, and emotional control. Recent data suggest that damage to this area impairs the ability to organize stimuli into meaningful sequences and to discriminate important differences between stimuli. There might also be some emotional dulling, distractibility, and memory deficits.

Temporal Lobes. As Figure 2 indicates, the temporal lobes are located on the side of the brain, just above the ear. Studies have shown that electrical stimulation of the temporal lobes (nonauditory areas) in conscious patients undergoing brain surgery for epilepsy will elicit extraordinarily vivid sensations and memories. The mechanism by which this occurs is unclear. Also, we cannot say with any certainty that the temporal lobe is the single site of memory function.

Association Areas. The functions of some areas of the cortex are not known. It was once believed that the association areas were important in forming mental connections between stimuli or between stimuli and responses. This suggestion was overly simplistic; the functions of these areas are still not clearly understood.

Subcortical Structures. The cortex is only a few millimeters thick, and most of the bulk of the brain is located beneath it. Subcortical brain structures are not involved in behavioral functions as sophisticated as the cortex. A highly developed cortex is a uniquely human characteristic; subcortical structures and the behaviors they deal with are shared by many animals. The structures lying under the cortex are not easily accessible and are therefore more difficult to study; therefore our information about them is less complete.

Corpus Callosum. The corpus callosum is a thick band of nerve fibers that connects the right and left hemispheres of the brain (see Figure 3). The brain is bilaterally symmetrical, one side being the mirror-image of the other. We each have a *dominant* and a *nondominant hemisphere*. The dominant hemisphere is on the side of the brain opposite our dominant hand. For example, if an individual is right-handed, his left hemisphere is dominant, and vice versa. One important function of the corpus callosum is to tell one hemisphere what the other is

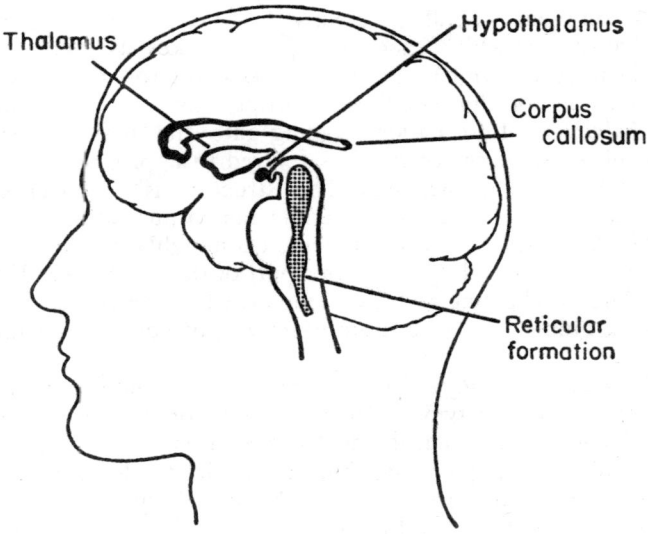

Fig. 3.   The Hypothalamus, Reticular Formation, Corpus Callosum, and Thalamus

doing. Information entering one half of the brain will cross over to the other half through the corpus callosum unless it has been severed, in which case the right side of the brain will not "know" what the left side is doing.

Experiments have been done with animals in which the corpus callosum and other smaller pathways between the hemispheres were cut and the animals were allowed to recover from the surgery. One eye was blindfolded and the animals were taught a task. Once they had mastered the task the blindfold was removed, the other eye was blindfolded, and the animal was tested again. It was found that nothing learned when the first eye was covered transferred to the other hemisphere: the animal had to start learning the task all over again.

There has been some recent evidence that the two hemispheres may be involved in different types of cognition. It is thought that the dominant hemisphere is largely concerned with logical, rational, and linguistic aspects of thought, and that the nondominant hemisphere is concerned with symbolic, nonlinguistic cognition (our so-called "creative" self). The nature of the mechanism by which each hemisphere makes its contribution to our total behavior is still obscure, as is the role of the corpus callosum in coordinating these contributions.

Thalamus. Information coming into the nervous system through most sense receptors is relayed to appropriate cortical areas through the thalamus. This structure is a collection of nerve-cell clusters located just under the corpus callosum.

The Cerebellum. The cerebellum is a highly wrinkled structure located beneath the posterior part of the cortex (see Figure 2). The cerebellum acts as a moment-by-moment correction system, aiding in the accurate execution of coordinated movements.

Reticular Activating System. The reticular activating system is composed of a network of neurons in the brain stem and upper spinal cord. These neurons deal not with ascending sensory or descending motor pathways, but rather with the level of arousal or alertness of the organism and the sensitivity of the sensory areas of the brain. (See Figure 3.)

The Hypothalamus. The hypothalamus, as its name indicates, is located just beneath the thalamus, just about in the center of the head. It has many, diverse functions. Parts of it are involved in hunger, thirst, and sexual behavior, behaviors typically involved in motivation and emotion. This structure has close ties with the endocrine system and the autonomic nervous system. Experiments have shown that electrical stimulation in certain parts of the hypothalamus is rewarding, while in other parts of the hypothalamus it is punishing. These effects are also noted when certain other subcortical structures are electrically stimulated. Some of the body's automatic functions are also controlled by this structure. These include heart rate, blood pressure, and the regulation of body temperature. (See Figure 3.)

The Limbic System. Figure 4 indicates the approximate location of the limbic system. It is thought that this group of subcortical structures is involved in the expression of emotion. When certain parts of the limbic system are experimentally destroyed, great changes occur in an animal's emotional reactions, depending upon the specific location of the damage. On the basis of these experiments, there is evidence that the limbic system is implicated in feeding, flight, aggression, and sexual behaviors.

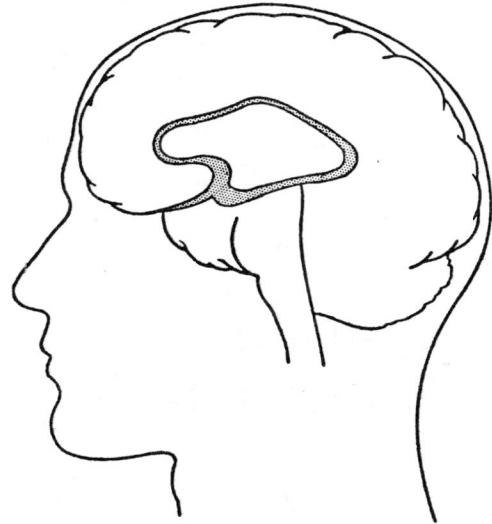

Fig. 4. The Limbic System. Shaded area shows approximate location of the limbic system as it might appear if the skull and rest of the brain were transparent. Its exact extent is not yet known.

This chapter has shown that biological factors affect behavior. The nature of this connection will be noted in several following chapters. It is difficult arbitrarily to separate aspects of heredity, maturation, and nervous system function from any psychological characteristics; any viewpoints adopting one perspective while excluding the other will necessarily be limited and incomplete.

Chapter 3

Learning and Conditioning

The ability to learn, to acquire information and use it at a later time, is probably one of the most valuable and sophisticated psychological capacities seen in man. A whole host of behaviors are learned, many of them quite different from one another. We learn such diverse things as communication skills, how to discriminate one red wine from another, how or whether men and women are expected to behave differently in society, or how to swim. All of these are quite complicated and worthy of careful study, but this chapter is devoted to far more simple types of learning.

Learning is a relatively permanent change in behavior that takes place as a result of rewarded practice. This definition does not strictly apply to improvements in behavior but to changes in general. It is something that we can only infer has taken place by observing changes in behavior in response to stimuli which previously did not elicit those changes.

The idea of reward or *reinforcement* is an important one. A *reinforcer* can be defined in different ways: it may be something that reduces one of the animal's drives as food reduces the hunger drive; it may be thought of as a bribe; it can be conceived of as an attention-getter. One of these definitions might apply to a specific learning situation better than the others.

The term *practice* commonly implies opportunity for repeated activity or trials; in definitions of learning it also might refer to a single event, since learning can occur with only a single experience. Although practice usually involves a conscious attempt to learn, there can be learning of which one is not aware.

Conditioning.   When, in a fairly restricted setting, an organism comes to respond to a stimulus in a way that it has not done previously, we can then say that the response is controlled by that stimulus. The experimental manipulations which bring this change about are collectively called *conditioning*. Conditioning techniques are effective in dealing with laboratory animals and human subjects as well as individuals with behavior disorders. They make it possible for organisms to acquire as well as discard responses. Trivial and meaningful behaviors can both be influenced by conditioning procedures. There are two kinds of conditioning: respondent and operant. Their similarities and differences will become clear in the discussion of each which follows.

RESPONDENT CONDITIONING

Respondent conditioning is also called *classical conditioning* or *Pavlovian conditioning* because much of the early research on this topic was carried out in the laboratory of the renowned Russian physiologist Ivan Pavlov (1849–1936). Pavlov became interested in conditioning while has was studying the digestive system of dogs.

An Example of Respondent Conditioning.   Imagine that you have a dog restrained in a comfortable laboratory harness, a supply of meat powder, and a bell. Before starting the experiment you ring the bell and find that the dog does not salivate. Your aim is to condition the dog so that he will salivate when you ring the bell without the meat powder being present. The purpose of the harness is to assure that the dog will be in a position to attend to the meat powder and the bell. Now you begin the procedure for respondent conditioning.

You ring the bell and place a bit of meat powder in the dog's mouth. The meat powder causes salivation. This ends the first trial.

After a pause you repeat the procedure, ringing the bell and then placing the bit of meat powder in the dog's mouth.

After, say, fifty such trials, you now ring the bell without giving the dog any meat powder. He salivates anyway. You have established a conditioned response; the response of salivation is conditioned to (controlled by) the sound of the bell.

Technical Terms and Procedural Details. The following are the technical terms in which respondent conditioning experiments are described.

1) *Unconditioned stimulus* (UCS)—A stimulus which before the experiment regularly elicits a measurable response. In the example above, the meat powder was the UCS.

2) *Unconditioned response* (UCR)—The response elicited by the unconditioned stimulus. In the example, salivation was the UCR.

3) *Conditioned stimulus* (CS)—A stimulus which before the experiment does not elicit any response resembling the unconditioned response, and which during the training is paired with the unconditioned stimulus. In the example, the conditioned stimulus was the bell.

4) *Conditioned response* (CR)—The response, very similar to the unconditioned response, which is made to the conditioned stimulus. In the example, the conditioned response was salivation. Upon close examination, the conditioned response is found to differ from the unconditioned response in certain minor details.

There are a few conceptual and procedural details concerning respondent conditioning that deserve attention. First, there is *timing:* the occurrence of the UCS and CS should be close together temporally if the conditioned response is to take place. They are typically separated by no more than one second, and separation by ½ second will yield best results. The animal will not learn the contingency between the UCS and the CS if they are separated by many seconds. This contingency seems to be very important early in a conditioning experiment while the role of reinforcements (UCS) is significant somewhat later.

Second, best results can be expected if the *magnitude* of the *CS* is great enough to capture and keep the animal's attention. A barely detectable CS will lead to poor conditioning.

Third, the *magnitude of the UCS* is important in establishing rapid conditioning. The larger the amount of meat powder used in the above example the more rapidly will conditioning take place.

Fourth, one important, noticeable change in the animal's behavior concerns its *attention.* Early in a conditioning experiment the animal will attend to many unimportant objects in its surroundings. The longer the animal remains in the experiment the more restricted will be the scope of its attention. Eventually, the animal is only attending to a very restricted subset of the potential stimuli in its environment; only a few stimuli become effective in the elicitation of the conditioned response.

The Strength of the Conditioned Response. There are four common ways in which the strength of the conditioned response can be empirically measured.

1) *Latency*—The amount of time elapsing between onset of the CS and onset of the CR. Short latencies are indicative of strong conditioned responses; long latencies, of weak conditioned responses.

2) *Magnitude of response*—Some conditioned responses, such as salivation, occur in different amounts that can be measured. Pavlov surgically placed a tube into the side of the faces of his experimental dogs so he could collect and measure saliva and thereby determine the strength of the conditioned response.

3) *Percentage of CR trials*—Respondent conditioning is shown to be stronger if the CR occurs on 8 out of 10 test trials than if it occurs on 6 out of 10 test trials. (The UCS is omitted on test trials.)

4) *Number of trials required for extinction*—The CS is presented repeatedly without being paired with the UCS, or the CS and UCS continue to be paired but at non-conditioning intervals. The CR weakens and eventually no longer occurs. The CR is said to be experimentally extinguished. The more such presentations are required before the CR fails to occur, the stronger the respondent conditioning was.

Spontaneous Recovery of the Conditioned Response. After a CR has been completely extinguished, if one then presents the CS after the passage of time, a moderately weak CR will result even though no conditioning was carried out after extinction.

Stimulus Generalization in Respondent Conditioning. If stimuli similar to the CS, but not identical to it, occur after conditioning has taken place, and the animal also responds to these stimuli, we then say that stimulus generalization has taken place. The response to the new stimulus will probably be weaker than the original CR. In testing an animal's stimulus generalization capacities, stimuli are varied along one dimension. If a light of a certain color is used in the original conditioning, a light of another color is used to test stimulus generalization.

(A tone would not be used if the original stimulus were a light.) The more similar the new CS to the original CS, the greater will stimulus generalization be, as indicated by the strength of the CR. If the initial CS was a red light, we can expect some generalization to occur to the sound the apparatus made when the red light was turned on, or, in the case of human beings, to the spoken word "red." A CS can be a complex stimulus.

Stimulus Discrimination in Respondent Conditioning. A subject can be conditioned to respond to one stimulus and not to respond, or to respond differently, to another stimulus. This is done by conditioning the desired responses while extinguishing the undesired ones.

For example, to train a dog to salivate to one musical tone and not to salivate to a lower musical tone, you would conduct a series of conditioning trials in which you sometimes sounded the higher tone, sometimes the lower. Sounding of the higher tone would be followed by the UCS, meat powder. Sounding of the lower tone would be followed by nothing. Thereby you would be conditioning the salivation response to the higher tone, while at the same time extinguishing any stimulus generalization to the lower tone. In due course, the dog would salivate only when the higher tone was presented.

Stimulus discrimination experiments have characteristics of the learning phenomena we have covered up to this point: the acquisition of a conditioned response, extinction, and stimulus generalization. Also, such experiments serve as good examples of the degree of control over behavior inherent in stimuli when used selectively and reinforced appropriately.

Also, stimulus discrimination experiments can tell us a good deal about an animal's sensory capacities. If a stimulus discrimination can be established between two stimuli, say two tones, we then know something about that animal's auditory discrimination capacities. When we cannot establish a stimulus discrimination, then we know something about the limits of an animal's sensory capacities. By using stimuli that are progressively more similar, we can determine the smallest stimulus differences to which that animal can respond.

Higher-Order Respondent Conditioning. In higher-order respondent conditioning, a second conditioned stimulus is paired with the original conditioned stimulus. Should the new CS come to elicit the same conditioned response after a number of pairings with the original CS, then higher-order respondent conditioning has taken place. This is called second-order conditioning. An example of second-order conditioning might go like this: a dog has been conditioned to salivate at the sound of a bell. The bell which was the CS in this experiment can now be used as the UCS in another experiment. A flash of light may be used as the CS which is to be conditioned to the response of salivation. The conditioning trials consist of presentation of the flash of light immediately followed by the ringing of the bell. After a number of these pairings in which the ringing of the bell is used to elicit salivation, the flash of light alone will now elicit salivation; higher-order conditioning has occurred.

Higher-order conditioning cannot be removed too far from the original, lower-order conditioning. As the new CS elicits the conditioned response, the capability of the original CS to elicit the same conditioned response is being extinguished at the same time. Higher-order conditioning is more difficult to achieve and maintain than lower-order conditioning.

Respondent Conditioning in Review. For some, the procedures and rationale of respondent conditioning are far too limited or artificial to be of much interest or significance. Because organisms are physically restrained to be sure they attend to specific, meaningful stimuli, analogous human applications are difficult to find. Because conditioned responses typically involve involuntary responses of the autonomic nervous system, it is again difficult to recognize examples of lower-order conditioning in our daily lives. Stimulus generalization and discrimination play an important role in determining the ways in which human conditioned responses ultimately are seen in our behavior, so that it is difficult if not impossible to determine the original conditioning experience. It is unlikely that our feelings or "gut-level" reactions can be attributed to some sequence of early experiences with any degree of certainty. Classically conditioned responses are not commonly seen in an organism's daily behavior in the form or magnitude that they are observed in the laboratory. Therefore such conditioning could be viewed as chiefly an experimental vehicle for the study of more complex learning processes.

OPERANT CONDITIONING

Operant conditioning is also called *instrumental conditioning.* In the design of operant conditioning experiments, the experimenter does not present the organism with a stimulus (UCS) that will elicit a response. Rather, the experimenter must wait until the organism displays a behavior already in its behavioral repertoire that he wishes to reinforce. By reinforcing this behavior, he increases the probability that the desired response will occur again. Some behavior on the part of the learner is instrumental to its receiving some reinforcing stimulus. This reinforcement may be something that the organism needs, or it may involve the termination of some stimulus unpleasant to the animal. Immediate reinforcement is an essential part of operant conditioning. It is thought that a behavior that has satisfying properties is one that the organism will try to make happen again; the satisfaction motivates the animal.

Certain concepts important in respondent conditioning are also important in operant conditioning. First, the reinforcement for a behavior must not be delayed too long after the occurrence of the behavior. Second, the reinforcement should be of sufficient magnitude and importance to the organism to have attention-getting properties sufficient to cause the learner to attend to aspects of its environment that are involved in acquiring reinforcement.

An Example of Operant Conditioning. You are using operant conditioning when you teach your dog to sit up by waiting until he sits up before you reward him with petting and praise. There was no UCS which elicited a UCR of sitting up. Thus one difference between conducting respondent and operant conditioning is that in respondent conditioning one uses a UCS to elicit the response, while in operant conditioning one waits until the desired response occurs. This of course implies a vigilant experimenter with specific requirements for reinforcement. The importance of this attentive attitude can be seen in those cases where the experimenter must gradually train an organism to perform a fairly complicated task.

Shaping. Some behaviors which experimenters wish to reinforce are extremely complex and would probably never occur in the learner's standard repertoire. The experimenter must therefore lead the animal along gradually through a series of behaviors which are incomplete steps on the way to accomplishing the complicated sequence. The experimenter will reinforce each such step, improving the chances that it will happen again. This process is called *successive approximation*. Each sequential behavioral step that is an approximation to the desired response is rewarded; all others are not, and are consequently extinguished. The experimenter *shapes* the animal's behavior through the appropriate dispensing and withholding of reinforcement.

For example, suppose that you decide to train your dog to retrieve your newspaper from your front porch. First you teach him that whenever you snap your fingers, this means that you will promptly throw him a small bit of meat. (This preliminary procedure makes it possible for you to use the snapping of your fingers as a signal immediately after the dog has done something for which he will be rewarded.) At first, the dog is likely to engage in "random" activity near you. Sooner or later he will happen to be pointed in the direction of the front door, and as this is a part of the behavior you would eventually like to condition, you snap your fingers and toss him a bit of meat. (For obvious reasons, this procedure will have a greater impact on your dog if he is hungry.) After this has happened several times, the dog will spend more time pointed in the direction of the front door. Now you must wait until he has taken a step or two toward it before snapping your fingers and rewarding him. After a few trials, when he is now at the door, you require him to successively point in the direction of the newspaper, walk to it, and retrieve it. It may be necessary now and then to throw in a few extra "free" rewards in order to keep this initially fragile conditioning from being broken down by other behaviors. By using techniques of successive approximation, you can reward behaviors that will serve as building blocks of the complex behavior you eventually wish to obtain.

These procedures have an obvious and powerful utility in working with people as well as laboratory animals. In teaching a child a motor skill such as swimming, it would first prove helpful to teach him something about breathing rhythm, then kicking, then arm stroking, then arm stroking with breathing, and finally the coordination of all of these skills.

The stepwise acquisition of skills and concepts as an educational tool has received wide popularity recently in the form of *programmed texts.* Allowing the learner the opportunity to master each successive aspect of a problem before attacking the next permits him to proceed at his own pace and eliminates the likelihood that he will be "left behind" by his classmates. The application of successive approximation techniques to education also encourages the educator to present material in a way that is more logical and direct than if he were using other methods. Since these procedures can train pigeons to play ping-pong or polar bears to play pat-a-cake, they can surely assist the fifth-grader with his math problems.

Experimental Extinction of Operant Conditioning. Responses learned through operant conditioning can be extinguished if the experimenter withholds reinforcement. Should you decide to stop rewarding your dog when he retrieves your newspaper, he will stop doing it. His behavior has been extinguished. The amount of time the extinction process takes is a good indicator of the strength of the original learning. Rapid extinction reflects an initially weak conditioned response.

Differences between Respondent and Operant Conditioning Experiments.

Question	Respondent conditioning	Operant conditioning
How much freedom does the organism have in the experiment?	Organism restrained in harness to insure exposure to CS and UCS.	Organism not restrained.
What is the nature of the response?	Automatic responses of the nervous system.	Responses emitted from standard behavioral repertoire.
When does response to be conditioned occur?	Experimenter presents UCS in order to elicit UCR.	Experimenter must wait to reward or punish until response, or an approximation of it, occurs.
What is reinforcement?	Presentation of the UCS shortly after the CS.	Reward or punishment of the response.
How is experimental extinction produced?	Repeated presentations of the CS *without* UCS or at nonconditioning interstimulus interval.	Withhold reward or punishment of response.

Spontaneous Recovery of Operant Conditioning. When reward or punishment of an operantly conditioned response is withheld, a point is reached when no response occurs for some time. The response is not completely extinguished, however, because now and then some further responses will occur.

Alternatively, if the subject is removed from the situation when responses first stop occurring, then when he is later returned to the situation, more responses will be made. Extinction may have to be repeated several times before spontaneous recovery is eliminated.

Stimulus Generalization of Operant Conditioning. After the subject has been rewarded for responding to a particular stimulus, he is likely to respond to stimuli resembling those which were present at the time of conditioning, although at a lower rate of response. For instance, suppose that a pigeon has previously been reinforced for pecking at an orange spot on the wall of its cage. If now the orange spot is replaced by a yellow one, the pigeon is likely to peck at the yellow spot, although the pigeon is capable of discriminating these two hues. As in the case of respondent conditioning, the more similar the new stimulus to the original stimulus, the stronger the response will be.

Stimulus Discrimination in Operant Conditioning. In stimulus generalization, the subject comes to respond in a similar but weaker fashion to stimuli resembling the stimulus used in original conditioning. In stimulus discrimination however, the subject responds to some stimuli and does not respond in any way to others. A stimulus discrimination task can be of two types. In one type, the stimuli to be reinforced and the stimuli to be extinguished are presented alternately, while in the other type they are presented simultaneously.

Suppose that your dog is just as likely to bark at the front door as at the back door when he wants to be let in. You decide to condition him to come only to the back door and bark when he wants to be let in. When he comes to the back door, you reward him by letting him come in. When he comes to the front door, you do not let him in, thus withholding the reinforcement in order to extinguish this response.

Operant Conditioning in Review. Operant conditioning appears to be of greater usefulness to humans than respondent conditioning. In order to establish an operantly conditioned response, the organism does not have to be restrained in some way. The phenomena for which operant conditioning has utility are numerous and diverse. Learning difficulties and discipline problems in children as well as bed-wetting are all areas where operant techniques are of great usefulness. The principles of operant conditioning are widely applicable; they can be used effectively by individuals of different backgrounds and training for many reasons specific to their own aims. Operant conditioning can be applied to the behavior of small and large groups of people as well as to individuals.

The role of the experimenter in operant conditioning experiments is a very directive one involving constant vigilance and control. Inconsistency or hesitance on the part of the experimenter can have a very negative impact on the outcome of the experiment. Once the subject learns the contingencies between stimuli, behavior, and reinforcement, any accidental change in the experimenter's actions will lead to a weakening of the developing conditioned response.

SCHEDULES OF REINFORCEMENT

Partial Reinforcement.   Up to this point, we have dealt with a situation in which every conditioned response is reinforced. However, this is not typical of everyday circumstances; organisms are very rarely on a continuous reinforcement schedule. Most situations involve organisms being reinforced on some occasions and not on others; that is, they are partially reinforced.

Four major types of partial reinforcement schedule are described below. First, however, it would be well to have a concrete situation in mind. Suppose that a hungry white rat is placed in a small cage through the wall of which protrudes a lever that he can push. Next to the lever is a small trough into which a bit of food can be put as reward. The animal has previously been conditioned to press the lever in order to be rewarded. This is a simple response that can be repeated at a high rate if need be, and the reward is sufficiently small that it can be given a number of times without significantly decreasing the animal's hunger. How is the animal's rate of lever-pressing affected by various schedules of partial reinforcement?

Fixed-Ratio Reinforcement.   In this partial reinforcement schedule, the number of times the rat has pressed the lever determines when he will receive reinforcement. The ratio of nonreinforced lever presses to reinforced lever presses is fixed. An animal on a 5 to 1 fixed-ratio schedule is rewarded only after every fifth response.

This schedule produces a high, steady rate of responding. If the ratio is gradually increased during the course of the experiment, one can reach a point at which the animal responds several hundred times quite rapidly before every reward. After a period of time, however, this ratio increase will lead to pauses in the rat's lever-pressing performance. The highest rates of steady responding can be produced with this schedule.

Fixed-Interval Reinforcement. In this partial reinforcement schedule, the amount of time between reinforced lever presses is constant, no matter how many such presses have occurred. Reinforcement is provided for the first response that occurs after a fixed interval of time. If our rat is on a two-minute fixed-interval reinforcement schedule, during that two minutes pressing the lever is not rewarded. After the two minutes is up, the first response which occurs thereafter is reinforced. There then follows another two-minute interval during which responding is not reinforced. The first response occurring after this two-minute interval is rewarded, and so on.

The rate of responding under this reinforcement schedule is very different from that found with the fixed-ratio schedule. Rate of response in the early portion of the fixed interval is negligible. As the end of the interval approaches, the rate of responding gradually increases, becoming highest at about the end of the interval.

Variable-Ratio Reinforcement. As implied by its name, in variable-ratio reinforcement the ratio of responses to reinforcements varies from one reinforcement to the next. For instance, an animal may be reinforced after 5, then 1, then 8, then 6, then 3, then 10 responses, and so on.

A steady, moderate rate of responding characterizes this reinforcement schedule. Behavior which has been maintained under this schedule is typically more difficult to extinguish than behavior which has been maintained under other schedules.

Variable-Interval Reinforcement. Under variable-interval reinforcement schedules, the temporal interval between reinforced responses varies from one reinforcement to the next. The behavioral effects of this schedule are similar to those of the variable-ratio schedule, except that the variable-interval schedule produces somewhat lower rates of responding than the variable-ratio schedule does.

AVOIDANCE LEARNING AND PUNISHMENT

Thus far we have dealt with conditioning procedures in which reward was used as reinforcement. Now we shall look at various conditioning principles in which the UCS has the quality of punishment.

Avoidance Conditioning. In the type of operant conditioning called avoidance conditioning, some signal appears which is soon followed by punishment unless the subject makes the required response. Punishment is avoided if the appropriate response is made in the allotted amount of time. The laboratory rat eventually learns to avoid punishment. However, in the first few trials there are a few aspects of the rat's behavior that make it difficult for it to learn to make the appropriate response. Upon being presented with punishment the first few times, electric shock for example, the rat may jump around, defecate, urinate, squeal, or simply freeze. The punishment-stopping response is usually made in an almost accidental way.

For example, an animal is in a cage which is divided in half by a wall in which there is a door. The floor of either half of the cage can be electrified to give the animal a mild but painful shock. A musical tone is sounded five seconds prior to the shock. If the animal crosses to the other half of the cage in less than five seconds, it avoids the shock. The same procedure can be repeated on the second half of the cage. In the early trials, the animal probably will not move to the other side of the cage before being shocked. The arousal caused by receiving the punishment of the electric shock may be important in the animal's "accidentally" running to the other side of the cage. The contingency between shock and the behavior which eliminates it becomes apparent to the subject. The subject eventually learns this contingency so well that it never receives the shock.

The animal can be taught to discriminate between two tones, one of which signals shock, the other of which does not. Avoidance conditioning is thus another procedure with which the sensory capacities of animals can be studied.

Escape Conditioning. In escape conditioning, no stimulus signals that punishment will ensue. But once the punishment has begun, an appropriate response will terminate it immediately. The animal eventually learns the connection so well that it will sustain only a fraction of a second of punishment on any trial. The absence of a warning signal is what differentiates the escape experiment from the avoidance experiment.

Avoidance and escape conditioning are often looked upon as different espects of avoidance learning in general. The subject must first learn escape behavior before it learns avoidance behavior. Both avoidance and escape conditioning deal with negative reinforcement, the situation in which the termination of a noxious UCS has reward properties. The termination and/or removal of the shock is rewarding to the laboratory rat.

Punishment. Punishment reduces the likelihood of behavior resembling the behavior that it follows. Behaviors that we wish to eliminate through the use of punishment often are maintained by rewards that the organism is reluctant to do without. The suppression of behavior through the use of punishment is not permanent. Punishment, or the threat of punishment, must be maintained as long as the behavior is to be suppressed. If punishment is too severe or distressing, a laboratory animal or a person will retreat from the setting in which attempts are made to change behavior. Of recent interest in psychology is the use of appropriately timed rewards and the selective *nonreinforcement* of behaviors to be suppressed. Nonreinforcement may take the form of totally ignoring or disregarding behavior. In these cases, punishments are not used, and the subject is less likely to withdraw from the setting in which attempts are being made to modify its behavior.

Punishment can play an indirect role in the permanent alteration of behavior, however. Punishment is sometimes used to suppress undesirable behavior temporarily, in order to permit the occurrence of desirable behavior, incompatible with the undesirable behavior, which can achieve the same goal. Here, punishment serves as a temporary expedient to suppress the undesirable behavior so that the desirable behavior can occur and be rewarded until it is well conditioned. This principle is illustrated by the procedures which some dog trainers use to teach a dog not to express its affection by jumping up on its master. The master squeezes the dog's front paws or steps on its rear paws with just enough pressure to cause discomfort but no real pain, thus mildly punishing the undesired behavior. As soon as the dog drops his paws to the floor, he is petted and praised. The slight punishment has suppressed the undesired behavior so that the desired behavior could occur and be rewarded.

OTHER ISSUES IN LEARNING

Reinforcement Hierarchies. Thus far we have concerned ourselves with conditioning experiments in which specific reinforcers, both positive and negative, have been used to enhance the chances of a behavior reoccurring. Other experiments have been done in which certain normally occurring nonreinforced behaviors have been shown to have rewarding properties for other normally occurring nonreinforced behaviors. Careful observation first had to be employed to determine how laboratory rats spend their time when they are not deprived of such common reinforcers as food, water, and the opportunity to exercise in a running wheel. Certain of the activities in the rat's daily behavior consume much of its time, others very little. The amount of time the rat spends in each activity from day to day does not change much. Behaviors that occupy a great deal of the rat's time have been found to have reinforcing properties for those behaviors which do not. Behaviors that have a high probability of occurring each day reinforce behaviors with a lower probability of occurring. An animal can be conditioned to increase the amount of time it spends in low-probability behaviors if it is rewarded with the opportunity to engage in a behavior that has a high probability of occurring among its daily activities. For instance, if a rat spends more time each day drinking than running, it can be conditioned to do more running if it is reinforced with the chance to drink. Similarly, a man who spends more time eating than exercising can be conditioned to do more exercising if he is reinforced with the opportunity to eat.

Serial Action versus Cognitive Maps. When a rat is trained to run through a maze to receive food, it must make an appropriate sequence of left and right turns. Its turns, and thus its behaviors, take place in a series. Many human and animal behaviors are made up of series of actions. Whether it be driving an automobile to work, building a piece of furniture, or writing a short story, an orderly series of thoughts and actions is involved. Yet does our behavior necessarily have this somewhat rigid, organized quality? Some learning theorists don't think so. They believe that knowledge of the "general direction" of any task is just as important as the step-by-step procedures involved in its solution. For instance, if while driving to work you encounter a detour, you can still get there even though your sequence of left and right turns has temporarily been changed. You realize that your destination is northeast of your starting point and you follow side streets heading in that general direction. It doesn't matter if you haven't been on those side streets before. Experiments with humans and animals indicate that this spatial organization of behavior is used in solving problems just as is the serial action interpretation.

THE NERVOUS SYSTEM AND CONDITIONING

It is difficult to attribute the acquisition of a conditioned response to the activity of a single, restricted segment of the nervous system. One commonly employed technique used to investigate brain function in relation to conditioning is *ablation*, or the removal of some of the brain tissue. A number of such experiments have been done. Here is a summary of their findings:

1) The more difficult a performance is for an animal to learn, the more this performance is subject to disruption by brain ablation.

2) In general, the larger the area of cortex ablated, the greater the disruptive effect.

3) Ablations which seriously impair sensory or motor function cause an initial impairment of performance, but subjects become very adept at using their remaining capacities to the fullest possible extent.

4) Ablation of an area which is not essential for conditioned behavior may nevertheless impair it, though not always permanently.

To illustrate the last point, it is not essential for a dog to have his visual cortex in order to learn to discriminate among light intensities, because he can successfully be conditioned to make this discrimination after ablation of all of his visual cortex. However, if a dog is first taught this discrimination, and then his visual cortex is ablated, the discrimination will be lost, though he can successfully be retrained to make this discrimination again.

In the previous chapter it was noted that a group of subcortical structures, the limbic system and the reticular activating system, were involved respectively in the expression of emotion and the level of alertness in an animal's behavior. In view of the fact that conditioning procedures require the animal to attend to significant aspects of its environment, the reticular activating system could be expected to play an important role in these procedures. Also, insofar as the noxious stimuli involved in avoidance and escape conditioning have an upsetting effect on the organism, the limbic system could be expected to be important in these kinds of conditioning. The ways in which these subcortical structures are involved in conditioning are not yet fully understood.

In studying the role of the nervous system in learning, several approaches have been used. Investigators have studied the physiology of learning by examining large areas of specific structures, single nerve cells, alterations in the functioning of synapses, and changes in the biochemical aspects of nervous-system functioning. No one method is the best. Information derived from all of these approaches is important and useful in our attempts to understand how stimuli can come to control behavior in conditioning experiments. We are still unsure about the role of the nervous system in learning, and further research is necessary to clarify the way in which the brain forms stimulus-response connections.

This chapter has dealt with highly controlled learning situations in which fundamental principles can be noted. However, conditioning does not occur only in experiments. In everyday life we form stimulus discriminations, find some of our behavior extinguished, sometimes punished, sometimes rewarded, and are operating under various reinforcement schedules provided by both nature and our associates.

Chapter 4

Memory, Forgetting, and Performance

MEASURING MEMORY

The results of the first systematic laboratory investigation of memory were published in 1885 by Hermann Ebbinghaus (1859–1909), while he was teaching at the University of Berlin. Ebbinghaus' book *On Memory* was a milestone in several respects. It showed that one of the "higher mental processes," memory, could be studied quantitatively in the laboratory. It reported the development of methods by which this could be accomplished and gave experimental results which have pretty well stood the test of time.

Ebbinghaus' work dealt with a specific type of memory, rote learning. Rote learning involves simple memorization, an activity involved in many aspects of learning. Although rote-learning techniques may not call for a great deal of intellectual sophistication, they are a good laboratory tool to help us see how people organize material that they are required to memorize.

Nonsense Syllables. One of the tools described in *On Memory* is the nonsense syllable. In designing his experiments, Ebbinghaus needed lists of verbal material to be memorized. But he could not use prose passages or lists of words because connected text or individual words would have associations attached to them. Some of these associations would be new, others old, some strong, others weak. For this reason, lists of words of equal length or prose passages of equal length would not have items equally difficult to learn. Some items would have certain meanings or certain thoughts attached to them and others would not. In order to get around this problem, Ebbinghaus used nonsense syllables—randomly chosen pairs of consonants with randomly chosen vowels inserted between them, for instance, SAZ, BUF, PIM. These are called *CVC trigrams*. Nonsense syllables provided him with stimulus materials of a very homogeneous nature: presumably, they would all be equally difficult to learn.

Using lists of nonsense syllables, Ebbinghaus performed his experiments, using himself as his experimental subject. He studied the effects of such factors as the amount of material to be learned, the temporal spacing of practice, the total amount of practice, and so on.

Two techniques used by Ebbinghaus to study memory which are still employed today are called serial anticipation and paired-associate learning.

In *serial anticipation*, a list of nonsense syllables is presented to the subject one syllable at a time, with the amount of time for each item held constant. After the subject has seen each item on the list once, he is asked to anticipate the presentation of each item by naming it. This procedure would be continued until the subject has correctly anticipated a certain percentage of the items on the list. This percentage, made known to the subject at the beginning of the experiment, is the criterion that he is expected to meet. The number of trials it takes the subject to reach the criterion is a measure of his learning performance.

In *paired-associate learning*, a list of pairs of nonsense syllables is shown to the subject, one pair at a time for a specified amount of time. The subject is asked to learn to associate one of the nonsense syllables with the other. Upon being shown the first, he is asked to supply the second, or vice versa. The order in which pairs are presented is changed from trial to trial so that the serial order in which the pairs occur does not supply the subject with a clue as to which associate is to follow. When the subject can correctly supply the nonsense syllable upon being presented with the first syllable in a specified percentage of the pairs, the criterion is reached. The experimenter again has a measure of the subject's learning performance.

Primacy and Recency Effects. Primacy and recency effects are very noticeable when a subject learns a serial-anticipation task. When items at the beginning of the list are learned particularly well, this is called a *primacy effect*. These items are supposedly learned more easily than items in the middle of the list because they are seen first. When items at the end of the list are learned well, this is called a *recency effect*. These items are said to be learned more easily because they are seen most recently. Primacy and recency effects typically have a significant influence on a subject's performance, as can be seen in Figure 5.

Curves of Learning and Forgetting.   Graphs showing the progress of learning may either rise or fall as performance improves, depending on how the ordinates of the graph are labeled. Improvement shows as a gradually rising line when accuracy or correctness of response is plotted as a function of amount of

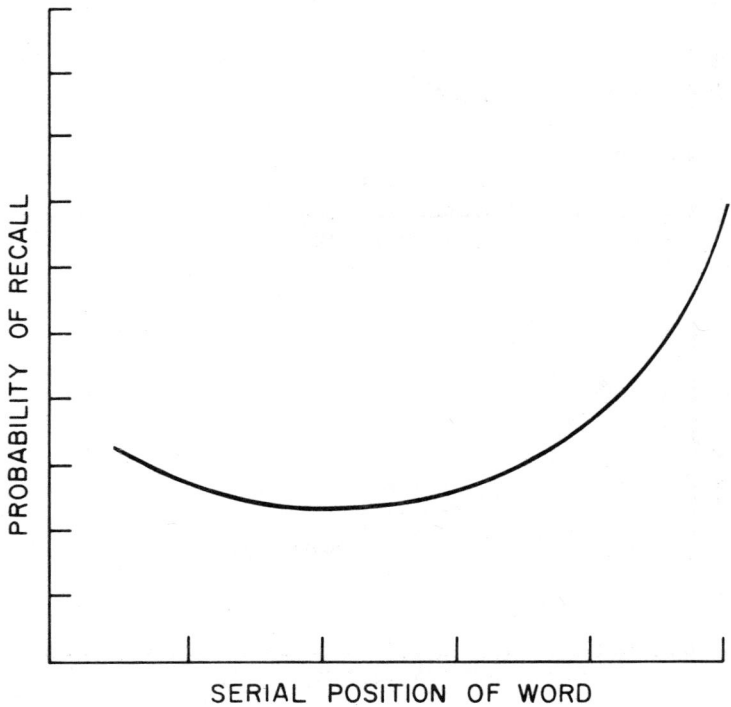

Fig. 5.   Serial Position Curve

practice. Improvement shows as a falling line when number or amount of errors is plotted against amount of practice (see Figure 6).

Forgetting curves are obtained when one of the measures of the amount retained (described below under "Retrieval Processes") is plotted as a function of the amount of time which has elapsed since the end of practice.

If one requires merely a single index of learning, rather than a learning or forgetting graph, one measures the number of

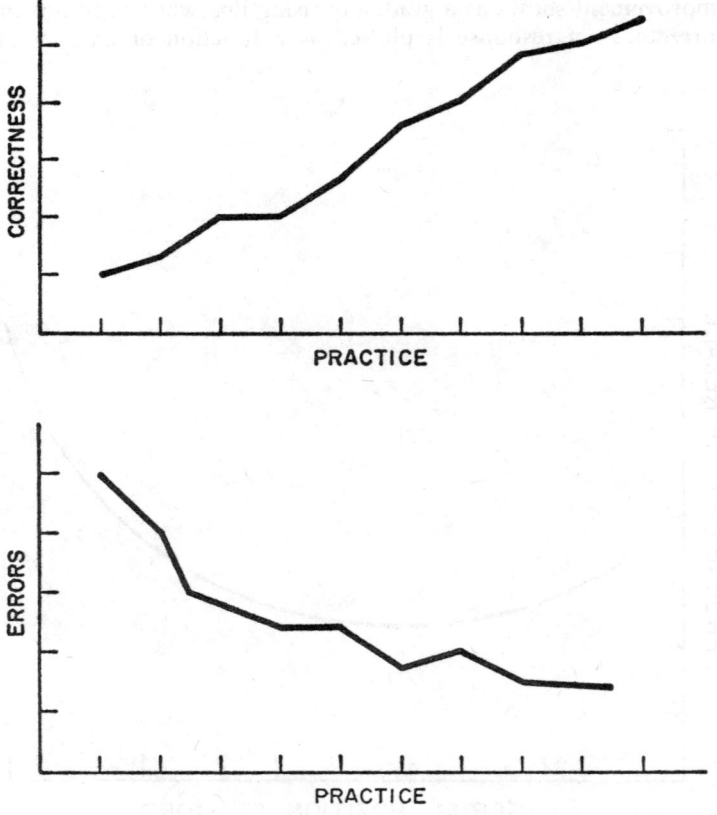

Fig. 6. Rising and Falling Learning Curves

trials or amount of practice required to reach a specified criterion of performance such as two successive errorless recitations, or 90% of perfect performance, or the like.

EFFICIENT LEARNING

Massed versus Distributed Practice. One of the most widely applicable principles of human learning is that short practice sessions with rest in between are more efficient than long or continuous practice sessions. This is true for many different kinds of tasks, including those both motor and verbal in nature. However, massed practice may be the superior technique when one is solving problems involving inductive thinking, such as puzzles for which one must discover the method which will yield a solution.

When verbal material is being memorized, as in a paired-associate task for example, distributed practice is often, though not always, advantageous. It is helpful when one has to organize and integrate his responses, as in memorizing foreign-language vocabulary lists. Also, distributed practice is more likely than massed practice to favor good motivation and to minimize fatigue.

Distributed practice has an even more strikingly beneficial effect on motor learning. In learning tasks requiring both strength and coordination, keeping fatigue during learning to a minimum will facilitate acquisition of the skill. Continuous practice will more readily lead to fatigue and thus loss of strength and impaired coordination.

Reading versus Recitation. Is it more efficient to read over and over the material which is to be memorized, or is it better to use the method of recitation, that is, very early in practice to attempt to recite the material from memory, referring to the material whenever one gets stuck? The recitation method brings about more efficient learning, in part because it concentrates the learner's efforts on the more difficult material which he has still not learned. It also permits the learner to impose his own organization on the material. Such recitation corresponds to one form of rehearsal. The more highly organized the material is to begin with, the less necessary will recitation be and the smaller the advantage obtained by using it.

Meaningfulness and Organization of Material to Be Learned. Material highly organized and meaningful to the learner is much more easily and quickly memorized than material which is not. Thus, a list of nonsense syllables is harder to learn than an equally long list of randomly chosen words. Poetry tends to be easier to memorize than connected text, as the meter and rhyme are useful organizing factors.

When material to be memorized lacks meaningfulness or organization the learner can use devices to impose his own organization on the material. One of these is *visualization*. If the learner mentally pictures an association to an item without meaning, he can later use the mental image as a cue to help him recall the meaningless item. Another device commonly used to help a learner organize large amounts of material to be memorized is called a *mnemonic*. Suppose that in studying for a history test you learned that ten events were critical in causing World War II. After having listed these on a sheet of paper, you make another list of the first word or few words in each. Then you memorize this list of cue words. When you can successfully list all ten critical events by using your list of ten cue words, you have successfully employed a mnemonic device.

Overlearning. One is overlearning when he continues to study the material beyond the point at which he has recited it once perfectly from memory. Naturally this requires more time in studying the material, but overlearning is efficient in the long run because overlearned material is less readily forgotten. In achieving mastery over some subject matter, some overlearning is usually necessary. Once material has been overlearned, it can also be forgotten, but at a slower rate than material not overlearned. A useful rule of thumb is that the amount of practice while overlearning should be from half the amount up to the same amount as was required initially to achieve the level of bare mastery. Further overlearning tends to yield diminishing returns. For example, if bare mastery has arbitrarily been defined as 90% of perfect performance, overlearning will of course result in continued improvement in performance.

Individual Differences in Learning. All individuals participating in learning experiments are not the same, nor do they have equal intellectual capacities or equal motivation to learn the material. What effect, if any, do these factors have on learning?

Verbal learning ability increases gradually from age five until the individual is in his early twenties. It then stays fairly constant until the individual reaches his early fifties. After that time, certain memory abilities begin to decline and the time pressures or "deadlines" involved in certain learning tasks are more apt to disrupt performance.

As might be expected, the scores individuals achieve on intellectual tests are related to their ability to acquire new information. Yet this relationship is not always trustworthy; learning ability and intelligence are not always predictive of one another. Several factors are involved. The incentive for learning is important, as are the individual's motives.

An individual's reasons for wanting to perform well on some learning task are diverse. The reward involved when performance reached a criterion might be one factor, particularly when the reward is large and important to the participant. The difficulty of the task and a subject's motivation have an interesting relationship to each other. When a task is very easy or when it is very difficult, too high a level of motivation (and thus arousal or excitement) will hinder performance. When a task is moderately difficult, a moderate amount of arousal will facilitate performance. This relationship can be described in graph form as an upside-down U-shaped function, as seen in Figure 7. The curved line in this graph shows that for tasks of differing degrees of difficulty, different amounts of motivation (arousal) are needed for best performance. Too much or too little arousal at the wrong time can lower performance. Individuals who "freeze" while taking an examination are far too aroused to perform well no matter how easy the material. A certain kind of memory error occurs in subjects experiencing a very high degree of motivation; this is called *confabulation*. If a subject cannot produce the correct response, he will make up one that seems appropriate.

Learning versus Performance.   Many unlearned as well as learned factors affect an individual's performance of learning tasks. Some of these unlearned factors might include the individual's motives for learning the task or the perceptual processes needed to learn it. Performance thus reflects a combination of both learned and unlearned influences, and it is difficult to tell what the latter are or when they are at work. Learning tasks must be designed in such a way that improvements in performance are directly attributed to the learning of specific information or skills.

Knowledge of Results.   Whether a learner is memorizing or is practicing a motor skill, he needs to be provided with imme-

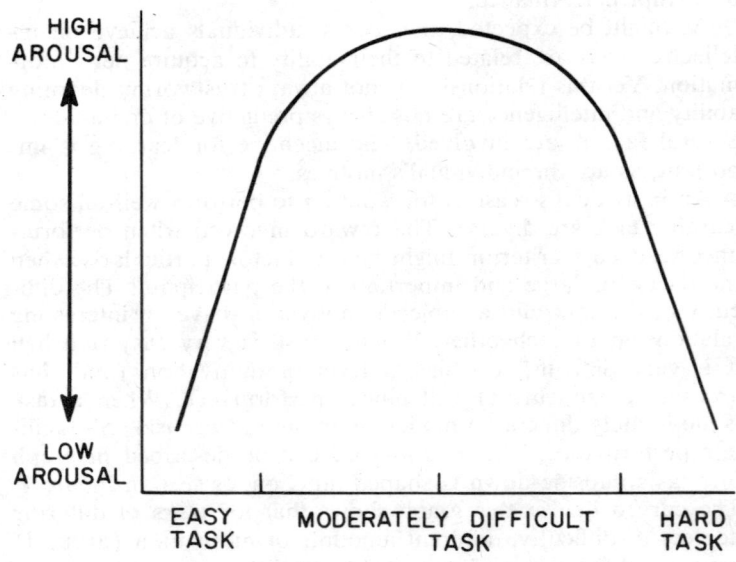

Fig. 7. Relationship between Level of Motivation, Difficulty of Task, and Performance

diate knowledge of results. That is, he needs to be informed of the accuracy of his efforts. Information that the subject has or has not met some criterion is, as you might expect, not as helpful as information concerning the magnitude of the error. Not only does supplying immediate knowledge of results provide the information necessary for correction of errors, but it has also been shown to have a beneficial effect on motivation.

RETRIEVAL PROCESSES

The most commonly used methods of testing for the amount remembered are the methods of redintegration, recall, recognition, and relearning. In considering each of these techniques, bear in mind that in memory experiments the storage of material and the retrieval of material from memory are related but somewhat different processes. It is quite possible to have some information stored in your memory but for one reason or another you may be unable to retrieve it on some occasion. Inability to retrieve does not indicate that the information is no longer in memory storage.

Redintegration. In *redintegration* experiments, the subject attempts to reconstruct some experience or sequence of actions he has observed. When one witnesses a crime, for instance, and is later asked to describe what he saw, he redintegrates his experience. Redintegration is difficult to study in memory experiments because there is often no one to verify an individual's description of an event. What distinguishes this method of studying memory from others is that a description of a specific *sequence* of occurrences is required.

Recall. In *recall* experiments, the subject attempts to repeat the performance which he previously had to learn. For instance, he attempts to recite "Kubla Khan" verbatim, or to park his car parallel in a designated parking place for the driving examiner. The accuracy of the performance is compared to some required standard. Few if any cues are given the subject, and for this reason recall tasks are fairly difficult.

Recognition. In *recognition* experiments, the subject attempts to pick out previously learned material from new material with which it has been mixed. For instance, the subject is shown 500 different photographs, and later 25 of these are removed and 25 new ones are substituted. The subject is then asked to specify which photographs have been added. Retention may be scored either in terms of percent of correct recognitions, or by means of a modification designed to compensate for guessing. In the latter case, percent correct can be computed as

$$\% \text{ correct} = \frac{100 \times (\text{no. right} - [p \times \text{no. wrong}])}{\text{total no.}}$$

where p is the proportion of correct answers expected due to guessing.

Relearning. In *relearning* experiments, something which was previously learned in a certain number of trials is later relearned. If the relearning takes fewer trials, this is evidence of retention, provided that there has been no increase in learning skill. The fewer trials needed for relearning, the more has been retained. Quantitatively, this relation is expressed in the *saving score*:

$$\% \text{ saved} = \frac{100 \times (\text{no. original trials} - \text{no. relearning trials})}{\text{no. original trials}}$$

By using this fraction, one computes the number of trials saved and compares it to the number of trials originally required. For instance, if original learning required 50 trials, and relearning required 30 trials, then there has been a saving of 20 trials, and this savings is 40% of the number of trials originally needed.

Faulty Retrieval. On occasion, we experience errors in retrieval because we don't have enough cues or because the cues that we have remind us of information similar but not identical to what we are trying to remember. One common example of faulty retrieval, known to almost everyone, is called the "tip of the tongue" phenomenon. Sometimes we begin a sentence with the intention of naming something—a person, a pet, or perhaps the name of a company. Yet we find that we can't, and feel frustrated because the word is on the "tip of the tongue." Studies of this phenomenon indicate that people often know the first letter of the word they are trying to remember, or the number of syllables in it, or its suffix. But other important cues are missing and attempts at retrieval are unsuccessful.

Another phenomenon, again known to almost everyone, involves a strong and strange feeling that we have been in a certain place when we know we have not. We falsely recognize the place as being familiar. This is called *déjà vu* experience. Certain characteristics of the new place, some which we may be unaware of, remind us of places we *have* been, or perhaps photographs we have seen, and these lead us to believe that the new place is familiar. The term *déjà vu* is French for "already seen."

TWO TYPES OF MEMORY

Short-Term Memory. The term *short-term memory* refers to our capacity to store or remember information only temporarily, seldom for more than thirty seconds. The capacity of short-term memory is only about seven items. For instance, when you use an infrequently called telephone number (seven digits) you typically have to look up the number each time you use it. If you reach a wrong number you find that you have to look the correct number up again; you can't remember it. Unless such material is regularly rehearsed it is "lost" from your short-term memory. Even brief distractions cause forgetting of material in short-term storage.

Long-Term Memory.   Information in long-term memory can stay there for years. When information is used repeatedly, it is likely to be stored in memory for a very long time. Also, memories of critical importance or great emotional impact are often never forgotten, even though they might concern events which occurred only once.

FORGETTING

In discussing the factors important in forgetting, it might be helpful to present a few general theories of the forgetting process. One of these perspectives is no more "correct" than the others; one may explain certain phenomena better than others in some situations and not in others.

Interference Effects.   Two common causes of forgetting are retroactive inhibition and proactive inhibition. In these processes, information acquired at one time interferes with retrieval of other information at another time. In *retroactive inhibition*, learning something interferes with the retention of something learned previously. For instance, suppose you spend an hour studying Spanish vocabulary, and then an hour studying French vocabulary. The studying of French will interfere with your retention of the Spanish.

In *proactive inhibition*, learning something interferes with the retention of something learned subsequently. In the preceding example, learning Spanish and then learning French, learning Spanish will interfere with the retention of the French.

(A useful mnemonic in keeping proactive and retroactive inhibition straight is to think of *pro*active inhibition as *pro*ceeding forward to the next thing learned; think of *retro*active inhibition as *retro*ating to act on the previous learning.)

The less similar the materials to be learned are, the less proactive and retroactive inhibition there will be. Therefore one would expect that these forms of interference could be lessened by decreasing the amount of related activity just before and just after learning. This is in fact the case. For instance, going to sleep right after learning decreases the amount of forgetting, as does decreasing the similarity of materials studied one after another.

The Memory Trace.   Another theory of forgetting suggests that when we learn or experience something, a physical change takes place in the brain. This change might involve an alteration in the connection between neurons or a chemical change in one or more neurons. Such a change is called a *memory trace*. Another name for a memory trace is an *engram*. When we forget something, the memory trace is assumed to "decay" or disappear. The idea of the memory trace is tentative, yet it is important in that it refers to brain processes in forgetting. The theory cannot account for our being able to retain certain motor skills and facts even when we have not had a need for them for several years. Nor can the theory explain elderly people's commonly retaining experiences that are many years old better than other experiences that occurred only a few days previously.

Repression.   Psychoanalysts have called our attention to motivated forgetting. Sometimes there is reason to think that an individual has not truly forgotten something, but at the time is unable to recall it because recall would arouse anxiety or guilt. (Note that in the concept of repression, the repressed material is never admitted to conscious awareness. Repression, therefore, is different from suppression. Suppressed material is material which was once conscious and which has been rejected from consciousness.) Repression is thought to be responsible for some cases of amnesia, in which the individual cannot recall his identity. (Another type of amnesia will occur in some instances of head injury, but this has nothing to do with repression.) The repressed memories are not wholly obliterated; the individual sometimes recovers them. Even though repressed memories are not consciously acknowledged, they still have the ability to motivate behavior, as we shall see in Chapter 10.

Meaningfulness.   Material which is meaningful to the learner is often found to be retained better than the material which he must learn by rote. For this reason, information without any organization is more difficult to learn and remember than organized material. For instance, students in a biology course are likely to remember biological principles better than biological terminology. One factor sometimes contributing to this is that remembering the meaningful material may require remembering fewer things than remembering rote material. As we have noted, subjects learning a list of nonsense syllables will remember those at the beginning and end of the list better than those in the middle. But if a meaningful word is inserted in the middle of the list it will be remembered at least as well as those at the beginning and the end.

Forgetting Curves. (Curves of retention.) A typical forgetting curve is shown in Figure 8. Shortly after the end of practice, the amount retained drops more rapidly than it does some time later. The extent of the drop varies considerably, depending upon interference effects and the meaningfulness of the material. It is typical to find that the rate of forgetting slows down with the passage of time.

CHANGES IN MEMORY

Qualitative Changes in Memory. Later recollections differ from earlier ones not only quantitatively, but also in qualitative ways. It is not yet clear how much the changes listed below

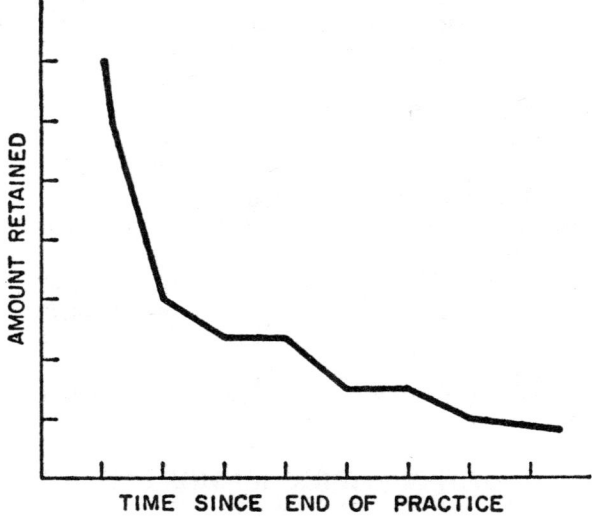

Fig. 8. Forgetting Curves

reflect changes that occur in memory as time passes, rather than being due to errors in perception and in recall. Whatever the reason, it is interesting that successive reproductions of pictures or of stories often show these changes:

Simplification—Structure is simplified and details are omitted.

Emphasis—Details which impress the individual as being striking or interesting are remembered well and emphasized.

Elaboration—New characteristics and details are invented, and some details originally present are changed into more familiar form.

TRANSFER OF TRAINING

Information learned in one situation can either facilitate or hinder performance in another situation. Transfer of training is said to be *positive* if previous learning increases the efficacy of learning or performing a different task. For instance, if you find that having learned Latin helps you learn French, positive transfer has occurred. Transfer of training is *negative* when previous learning decreases the efficacy of learning or performing a different task. For instance, if you find that having learned to drive in an American-built automobile with an automatic transmission confuses you when you try to learn to drive a foreign car with a manual transmission, negative transfer has occurred.

Positive transfer is to be expected when the same responses previously learned are to be made to new stimuli. For instance, a boy who has practiced ping-pong should show positive transfer when he begins to practice tennis.

Negative transfer is to be expected when the same stimuli now require new responses which compete with, or are opposite to, the responses originally learned. For instance, one would expect difficulty in introducing a group of ladies by their married names for the first time if one had previously known them well by their maiden names.

Transfer of training, positive or negative, depends on the degree of similarity of the stimuli.

"PHOTOGRAPHIC MEMORY"

Perhaps you know someone who has a "photographic memory." These people seem able to take a "mental photograph" of anything they see and then refer back to it at a later time to extract minute, specific details. This very rare ability is thought not to be a type of memory at all; it is called *eidetic imagery*. People with eidetic imagery do not need to observe something for very long in order to get this effect. These individuals can "photograph" pictures, scenes, or pages of print and supply perfect recall of what they have seen. Little is known about the mechanisms of eidetic imagery, nor do we know what percentage of the general population has it. It is thought to be more common among children than adults.

Chapter 5

Motivation

Motives and Behavior. There are certain things that we need in order to stay alive; among these are food, water, and a reasonably constant body temperature. There are other things we feel we must have, but are not essential to our survival. In each case, we see behavior directed toward some goal and infer the existence of corresponding motives. When motives are involved in the survival of an individual or of the species, they are called *biological* or *primary motives*. When motives are learned through training or imitation, they are called *acquired* or *secondary motives*. Both kinds of motivation are often involved in behavior. For example, a formal dinner party involves both the biological hunger motive and acquired social motives.

What is the sequence of events concerning the ways motives originate, the way they change, and the way they affect our behavior? It is thought that when we perceive some deprivation or need, we develop a *drive* to reduce the deprivation or need. Such a drive serves to energize and direct our behavior. If we are deprived of opportunities to achieve or accomplish our goals (as is the case in some occupations), we recognize a drive to achieve, realize that it is not being satisfied, and thus may become bored or frustrated. This need might become obvious as we begin to look around for another job. In either case, we cannot see a drive, but we infer that it exists because of the way an individual behaves. Motivated behaviors keep us "in balance" biologically and psychologically by helping us do something about our needs. Psychologists debate as to whether the terms "motive" and "instinct" (as defined in Chapter 2) are equivalent.

There is still another way to view motivated behavior. Some psychologists believe that deprivations and needs are not as important as certain aspects of the environment having motivational properties called *incentives*. Incentives may direct and energize behavior when no biological deprivations or psychological needs are perceived. If an individual feels that he is achieving his goals in his job, the added incentive of a merit pay-raise above his cost-of-living raise might motivate him to set still higher goals and try to reach them.

PRIMARY MOTIVES

Pain Avoidance. Pain starts to be felt at approximately the level of stimulation which begins to cause damage to bodily tissues. At this point the organism typically is aroused to remove itself from the painful situation. Sometimes the escape from painful stimulation is a matter of automatic reflex action, as when one jerks his finger away from contact with a hot stove. At other times the behavior which avoids pain has been learned, as when one takes precautions to avoid sunburn. All individuals are not equally sensitive to painful stimuli and a few are born "pain blind," being very insensitive to stimulation which is highly painful to most people and always causes tissue damage.

Maintenance of Constant Body Temperature. There is a comparatively narrow range of body temperatures within which the chemical reactions of the body take place efficiently. Some of the body's defenses against undue temperature variation are reflexive in nature, such as the perspiration which begins when the temperature at the hypothalamus begins to rise, or the shivering when it begins to fall. There are also learned behaviors which contribute to maintaining desirable body temperature, such as the putting on of a sweater or the turning on of an air-conditioner.

Thirst. When the body contains less than its usual amount of water, there is a tendency to dryness of the tissues. There are different ways in which this can happen; we lose water when we excrete it through our kidneys and when we perspire. It was once thought that dryness of the mouth and throat served to signal the need for water. While it is true that a sip of water helps alleviate our thirst, it is now clear that more complicated mechanisms are involved in the behavioral regulation of the water content of the body. We know that cues for thirst come from the hypothalamus as well as the mouth, throat, and stomach.

An illustration of the phenomena which have to be accounted for is provided by an experiment on dogs which had been operated on, the esophagus having been cut and the upper and lower ends of it having been brought out to the surface of the body so that the water the animals drank could not get to the stomach. When these dogs needed water, they drank an amount proportional to that which they needed, and then stopped, even though the water never got to their stomachs to relieve their bodily needs. However, if the needed water was first placed directly into the stomach, then how much a dog drank depended on how long prior to that the water had been put into his stomach. If he was allowed access to drinking water immediately after water had been put into his stomach, he drank the same amount he would have if no water had been placed in his stomach. If drinking was delayed 10 minutes, he took some water, but not as much as he otherwise would have. If he were allowed access to the drinking water only 15 to 30 minutes after water had been placed directly in his stomach, he did not drink at all. These findings indicate that the normal animal drinks about the right amount of water to satisfy his bodily need, and then stops before his body "knows" that the deficit has now been allayed.

If thus appears that there are two separate questions to be answered: what starts an animal drinking when it needs water, and what stops it when it has had enough?

Certain portions of the hypothalamus (see Chapter 2) play a role in initiating the onset of drinking. When there is less than the usual amount of water in the body, changes in the blood and other body fluids take place. Their volume decreases and they contain more sodium. The hypothalamus has cells that are sensitive to these changes. The hypothalamus works together with the pituitary gland (see Chapter 2) to regulate the amount of sodium in the body. When the body's sodium concentration gets too high, cells in the hypothalamus "notice" this and cause the pituitary gland to secrete a hormone into the bloodstream.

This hormone acts on the kidneys in such a way that less urine is produced and more water stays in the body.

Sodium sensitivity of the hypothalamus is suggested by an experiment on goats in which it was possible to apply to the appropriate part of the hypothalamus a drop of salty water slightly higher in concentration than the body fluids. Although the goats always had unlimited access to water, and therefore presumably had little need for it, application of a single drop of salty water to the appropriate part of the hypothalamus resulted in immediate and copious drinking of water, often several gallons. This indicates that the hypothalamus plays a role in initiating water-drinking when the body needs water.

Decreased blood volume is monitored by the kidneys, which in turn secrete a hormone. This hormone influences the hypothalamus to cause blood vessels to constrict to accommodate decreased blood volume. The hypothalamus also sends a message to the cortex to initiate drinking behavior.

The mechanisms by which water drinking behavior is stopped, before the water ingested has had time to be distributed throughout the body, are not yet clear.

Hunger. As in the case of thirst, both cues from the body and the functioning of the hypothalamus play a role in hunger as a motivator. Contractions of the stomach when it is empty were once thought to be the most important hunger cue. However, we know now that other mechanisms must be involved. Animals and human beings have hunger feelings when their stomachs have been surgically removed and food passes straight to the intestines, with no stomach to produce contractions.

Another suggested hunger cue concerns a lowered amount of sugar in the blood. In one experiment, blood from a food-deprived dog was injected into a normal dog. The normal dog then began to have stomach contractions similar to those in hungry dogs. These stomach contractions stopped when blood from a well-fed dog was then injected into the normal dog.

Other suggested hunger stimuli include the amount of fat and certain hormones in the bloodstream. While the taste and smell of food are of obvious importance in our eating habits, they do not play a significant role in our monitoring of food intake.

The hypothalamus plays a part in the control of eating. If tissue is destroyed in the ventromedial parts of the hypothalamus (on the underside of this structure along the midline of the brain), there is a considerable increase in the amount the animal eats. The animal may even become three times its normal weight. It is thought that cells in the ventromedial area are sensitive to the amount of stomach fullness. On the other hand, destruction of appropriate tissue in the lateral parts of the hypothalamus results in decreasing the amounts animals eat. It thus appears that the lateral areas are involved in initiating eating, while the ventromedial areas have to do with the cessation of eating. Further support for this theory comes from the fact that electrical stimulation of these areas by means of electrodes implanted in the hypothalamus results in the expected behavior.

Body temperature is another cue believed to be involved in hunger. Cells in the lateral hypothalamus seem to alter their rate of activity when their temperature is lowered, while cells in the ventromedial hypothalamus alter their rate of activity when their temperature is raised. When the weather is hot we typically feel like eating less, and when it is cold we often want to eat more.

Secondary motivational aspects of hunger are also important. Social customs and dining schedules play a role in what we eat, how often, and when.

Specific Hungers. We don't eat simply because we need nutrients in food. Out diet is determined both in quality and amount by a combination of personal and cultural preferences. In some animals, preferences are innate. Laboratory rats, for instance, prefer slightly salty drinking water and food. Suppose an animal or baby is allowed to select freely among various foods (cafeteria-style) and to eat as much or as little of each food as it wants to. In some cases, though not all, it may eat only one kind of food for days, then switch to another kind and stay with that for several days; but in the long run it may take in the proportions and variety of foods necessary for a soundly balanced diet. Furthermore, if for some reason there is an unusually high bodily need for some particular dietary component, the animal or baby may ingest unusually large quantities of food containing that item, even if that food is regarded as comparatively unpalatable.

Learning is important in acquiring aversions to certain foods. If a rat eats a small amount of poison, enough to make it sick but not kill it, it will avoid the poison thereafter. The same thing happens with people. If you are unaccustomed to eating raw fish, then eat a small piece and subsequently become ill, afterwards you will probably avoid raw fish and perhaps even cooked fish as well.

Unfortunately, specific hungers can be interfered with by preferences and habits, so that self-selection of diet does not guarantee a nutritionally well-balanced diet for each and every individual.

Sleep. We all need to sleep, but in differing times of the day. Our sleep habits, while determined by need, are also affected by our work schedules and age. In the course of development, we change our sleep schedule and requirements. Newborn infants sleep several short periods each day. The young child may need one or two naps in addition to a number of hours of sleep at night. Adults typically need much less sleep than children.

Our sleep is not all deep sleep. At the beginning of a sleep period we are in light sleep. We gradually progress to deeper sleep, and toward waking progress to lighter sleep again. Depth of sleep can be monitored by recording brain activity with electrodes pasted on the scalp. This activity is amplified and recorded by a machine called an electroencephalograph.

The biological mechanisms involved in the need to sleep are still obscure, although we know that the body has a "biological clock" which influences our daily sleeping and waking rhythms as well as other bodily processes. It has been thought that the need for sleep might result from an accumulation of some sort of chemical products in the blood as a consequence of bodily fatigue. Research in this area has discovered a chemical that may be implicated. When this chemical is injected into alert rabbits, they quickly fall asleep. It is not yet known how this chemical is produced in the body or how it works. The reticular activating system apparently plays a role in waking and sleeping, but many details are still unclear.

When people are deprived of sleep for a long period of time they become disoriented, complain of headaches, have difficulty concentrating, show some memory impairment, and sometimes have hallucinations.

Sex. Sex hormones are secreted by male or female sex glands into the bloodstream. These hormones affect both appearance and behavior, playing a role in both the development of the physical characteristics of the two sexes and their sexual motivation and responsiveness. The lower the organism is in the evolutionary scale, the greater becomes the role played by sex hormones in motivation. This is shown by the decrease in sex motivation when these glands are surgically removed. In lower animals, sexual behavior is rigidly controlled by these hormones. Within a single species, all animals display the same sexual behavior. As one proceeds higher in the evolutionary scale toward man, sex hormones have less influence on sexual motivation, and a larger role is played by learning, habit, and custom. This accounts for the variety of human sexual behavior. Incentive stimuli are particularly important in humans also, more so than perceived drives to reduce some physiological need. Unlike a hungry or thirsty animal, an animal can survive in a longstanding state of sexual deprivation.

Much of the nervous system is involved in sexual behavior, although the role of certain brain areas in sexuality varies across species. The cerebral cortex, hypothalamus, spinal cord, and autonomic nervous system all play a part. As you might expect, the higher one goes on the evolutionary scale, the more important the cerebral cortex is in sexual behavior.

SECONDARY MOTIVES

We are motivated by many things that are not needed for survival, but which are powerful motives nevertheless. As in the case of primary motives, *learned* or *secondary motives* both energize and direct behavior. We will also see in Chapter 10 that it is quite possible to have a secondary motive and not know it; it can be unconscious. Important in the study of learned motives are the goals we choose to strive for and the reinforcements we derive by reaching these goals.

When we see a man working hard to accumulate money or earn prestige, we infer from his behavior a corresponding motive. There is no reason to think that a desire for money or prestige is an innate characteristic of all humans. How, then, is such a motive acquired?

Social Learning.   One way we acquire motives is from the impact of our social environment. In part, we learn what behaviors our society rewards by performing those behaviors and being reinforced for them. Another way we learn which behaviors are rewarded by observing other people. Such learning-by-observing stresses our ability to regulate our actions and evaluate our progress. Society will sanction or punish our goal-directed behavior; and we, in turn, continue toward our goal, or perhaps choose another. Once we evaluate our reinforcements, we are or are not motivated to continue acquiring such reinforcements.

Psychoanalytic Approach. Another way we acquire motives has been suggested by Sigmund Freud (1856–1939), the noted Viennese physician who developed a theory of personality and method of treating mental disorders called *psychoanalysis*. Psychoanalysis is also a theory of human motivation. Freud speculated that humans have two innate motives, sex and aggression. Yet society discourages the fully open expression of these motives. We therefore block their direct expression by a mechanism called *repression*. Once we have done this, these motives still appear in our behavior, but in disguised ways. They may appear in our dreams or in slips of the tongue. On occasion, it may be possible for others to infer from our behavior the existence of motives of which we are not conscious. In a given case, it may be unconscious motives which are responsible for behaviors with which we surprise ourselves, or which interact with our conscious motives to result in behaviors that are either more vigorous or more hesitant than seems appropriate.

Cognitive Approach. Still a third perspective on human motivation involves a cognitive approach. This view has a humanistic orientation and places little emphasis on the role of reinforcement or unconscious motives. One theorist, Abraham Maslow (1908–1970), has suggested that we rank-order our motives. We first see to our biological needs, need for feelings of safety, and need to be accepted by others. After we have taken care of these, we try to satisfy our motives to acquire esteem, to comprehend, and to see order in our world. Then Maslow suggests that we have a motive to become *self-actualized*, to realize our full potential and become the best people that we can. We therefore establish a hierarchy of motives, satisfying our biological before our psychological requirements. As you can see, the cognitive approach puts emphasis on our knowledge of where we have been in our growth, where we are, and where we are going. Realistic perceptions of ourselves and free will are major characteristics of the cognitive viewpoint.

Social Motives. Whether we view acquired motives from the learning, the psychoanalytic, or the cognitive viewpoint, these motives are most important in social situations. It is sometimes proposed that all social motives develop from one or another postulated universal human motive such as aggression, competitiveness, or the need for power over people and our environment. The fact that there are a number of rival theories concerning a postulated basic motive suggest that there is no overwhelming evidence in favor of any one theory. At present it is not clear how many different social motives there are nor how independent of one another such motives may be. However, the following list (adapted from H. A. Murray) gives an idea of the range of motives believed to exist to at least some degree, at one time or another, in man. Such motives include the desire for:

1) achievement and accomplishment
2) aggression
3) avoidance of feeling inferior
4) avoidance of physical injury
5) deference to others
6) dominance of others
7) exhibitionism
8) friendship
9) helping those who are weaker
10) imitation
11) independence
12) orderliness
13) overcoming defeat
14) play
15) receiving sympathetic help
16) rejection of others
17) self-abasement and passive acceptance of punishment
18) self-defense against criticism and blame
19) sensuality
20) sexual activity
21) understanding of general principles
22) avoidance of success

Although some of the foregoing motives are contradictory, it is perfectly possible for them to be present in an individual at the same time to one degree or another. For example, a boxer's motives may include both aggression and avoidance of physical injury; another man may desire the friendship of others and yet, through fear that they will not respect him, reject their offered friendship. Also, different motives become important in an individual at different times. It should be noted, moreover, that human behavior can become independent of the motive that first caused it. For example, if you have been poor and through long, hard work you acquire wealth, even though you no longer have to work, you are likely to continue to work. This is called *functional autonomy*. The behavior that was once motivated becomes motivating.

Recent research has indicated that many women have as a motive the avoiding of success. Although this appears strange, it is thought to be a fairly stable personality trait. Such a motive has been suggested because women often are hesitant and reluctant to excel in occupations in which they compete with men. They fear that they will jeopardize their relationships with men if they do better than them in competition.

MIXED CASES

Some motives do not fit neatly into either the category of acquired motives or of motives serving biological needs. Perhaps this is because we do not understand the development of these motives very well, but mention of a few such cases seems in order. In each of the following cases it will be difficult to determine the degree to which the behavior in question is acquired or physiologically motivated.

Curiosity. Humans and laboratory animals like to look at and manipulate novel stimuli. This is intrinsically rewarding. The monkey will learn a task which gives him no other reinforcement than a look into another room. The novel stimuli which reward curiosity need never have been associated with another reinforcement, and it is also hard to see how they can reward a biological need in the same direct sense as food or water do. The idea of curiosity or investigation is also apparent in the play of infants as they manipulate, disassemble, and reassemble their toys.

Sensory Stimulation. As we just noted, there seems to be a motive to experience novel stimuli. Research has shown that there appears to be a motive to experience stimuli *in general*, because when people are experimentally deprived of normal sensory input they find the situation highly aversive. These subjects are placed in quiet rooms, wear cardboard cylinders around their arms and hands, translucent plastic around their eyes, and are required to remain motionless. They cannot see shapes, hear sounds, touch objects, or receive sensations from moving limbs or contracting muscles. Many subjects find the experiment intolerable after two or three days, even though they are well paid for taking part. During the test, some of them experience visual hallucinations and most cannot concentrate clearly; many become bored and highly irritable.

Contact Comfort and Mothering Behavior. Almost all mammalian infants enjoy being cuddled by their mothers; they seek her embrace when they are frightened or distressed. Why does the mother have these reinforcing characteristics?

The following experiment demonstrates the concepts involved in contact comfort. Two artificial monkey "mothers" were constructed, and each was put into a cage with a live infant monkey. The first dummy was constructed of rough wire—clearly an unsatisfactory material for cuddling. However, affixed to the rough model was a nursing bottle from which the first baby monkey received its milk. The second mother-substitute was made of terry cloth. This model was soft and appealing to the touch, but no arrangements were made for it to supply milk.

When frightened, the two baby monkeys reacted very differently. The first monkey would ignore the wire dummy, and would cower on the floor of his cage, covering his face and rocking back and forth. The second monkey, on the other hand, would run to his terry cloth "mother" and embrace it, peering over its shoulder now and then to see what was going on. Clearly the contact comfort from the terry-cloth mother was more satisfying to the one baby monkey under these circumstances than the availability of milk attached to the rough dummy was to the other baby monkey.

A mother does not have to act like one in order to survive herself—but if she doesn't the species won't survive. Caring for their young is one of the most powerful motives of mammalian mothers as well as species lower on the evolutionary scale, such as birds. Depending on the animal, maternal behavior may be instinctive (see Chapter 2), hormonal, learned, or some combination of these. A mother rat will endure the pain of an electrified cage floor to retrieve her young. She will not cross the electrified floor as often to obtain food or water if she has been deprived of these.

The pituitary gland secretes a hormone called *prolactin* that is important in mammalian mothering behavior. This hormone is responsible for starting and maintaining milk secretion when offspring are born. Experiments have been done in which virgin female rats or (strangely enough) male rats have been injected with prolactin. They will then build nests out of shredded paper supplied by the experimenter and will begin to care for young rats born of other mothers.

In the above experiments with infant monkeys and mother substitutes, it should be noted that female infants raised with either sort of substitute mothers did not display normal maternal behavior when they first became mothers. These mothers ignored or sometimes actually harmed their offspring. In subsequent pregnancies they tended to act more like normal mothers, supposedly having had a chance to learn what mothering entails.

As there probably are not any human instincts, human mothering behavior is believed to be dependent on learning and the action of prolactin. Other female hormones also are known to affect a woman's behavior at the time of childbirth and shortly afterward.

BRAIN STIMULATION

Electrical stimulation of certain portions of the hypothalamus and nearby structures is rewarding; electrical stimulation of other areas deep in the brain has the same effects as punishment. Animals with stimulating electrodes implanted in the former areas will learn and do work for no other reward than a weak electrical stimulation. In fact, such an animal will spend hours repeatedly pushing a lever which has been connected to deliver brief electrical stimulation of this sort. It appears that the animal never tires of such a reward. In contrast, an animal with a stimulating electrode implanted in a "punishment" area of the brain will press such a lever once and not return to it.

Similar electrode implants have been carried out on human subjects, particularly those experiencing severe forms of depression and some types of extreme mental disturbance. A console is worn by these individuals so that they can stimulate certain areas of their own brains. Needless to say, this is a very unusual therapeutic procedure, one employed when all other available means have been tried and found ineffective.

The identification and measurement of motives, whether innate or acquired, may well be the most difficult and challenging task of psychology. As you have seen, many different areas within psychology are concerned with human motives, and it seems that such an interdisciplinary approach is necessary. In the field of motivation more than in any other, increased knowledge from experimentation will greatly increase our understanding of everyday behavior.

Chapter 6

Emotion

Emotions are very important aspects of our behavior. Some of them are apparent while others are very subtle. We often wonder why we become angry or fearful or happy. Emotions can be motives or goals of our behavior. Emotions can be adaptive or disruptive in terms of our performance. Emotions change as we become older, suggesting that maturation may be involved. Many questions about emotion have not yet been answered by psychologists. In this chapter we shall consider some of the fundamental points that have been established so far.

DEFINITION OF EMOTION

Describing meaningful personal feelings with words is difficult, and for this reason a satisfactory, widely applicable definition of *emotion* is difficult to arrive at. It is hard to find characteristics that are common to all of the many states which are referred to as emotional. Like motives, emotions energize and guide behavior. Emotional behavior is usually observable.

In this chapter we consider the following aspects of emotion: 1) physiological changes occurring during emotion; 2) behavioral expression of emotion and the role of cognition; 3) learning and emotion; 4) emotions and human performance.

PHYSIOLOGICAL CHANGES DURING EMOTION

Fear and Rage.   Most of our knowledge of physiological occurrences during emotion pertains to fear and rage aroused in laboratory animals. These two emotions are not difficult to arouse in animals, and the resulting physiological changes are large and easy to measure. It should be kept in mind that the behavior discussed resembles that seen in human beings under similar circumstances, though it would be anthropomorphism to claim that the situations are identical. (Anthropomorphism is the ascribing of human motives and emotions to things which are not human.)

It might also be useful at this point to discriminate between fear and anxiety, a frequently reported human emotion. *Fear* is usually attributed to a specific, recognizable, observable threat of some kind. *Anxiety* is not so specific; it is a diffuse feeling of uneasiness the cause of which we may not be aware. For this reason, anxiety is generally more difficult for a person to deal with. *Rage* may be defined as the overt expression of uncontrolled anger.

Although there is some evidence suggesting that there may be certain quantitative differences among the physiological events during fear, anxiety, and rage, for our purposes we may consider these together. In outlining physiological changes during emotion, we should note that there has been considerable debate over whether these changes are the *causes* or *results* of our emotions.

The "Fight or Flight" Reaction.   The physiological reactions described below have been named the "fight or flight" reaction, since they prepare the organism for the sudden violent activity which will occur when there is fighting or fleeing. The autonomic nervous system (see Chapter 2) is involved in assisting the body to meet these emergency needs and to return to normal afterwards. The hypothalamus and limbic system are also involved in fear and rage, and with the cerebral cortex play a role in directing the emotional behavior of the organism. The physiological reactions involved in fear and rage are as follows:

1) The activity of the digestive system stops. Contraction of the stomach and intestines ceases, and salivation ends. Blood is channeled away from the stomach and intestines and toward the brain and skeletal muscles. Thus, energy is not wasted on functions which are of no immediate help during the crisis.

2) Heart rate speeds up; some blood vessels expand and others contract in such a way as to shift blood supply away from the digestive system and toward the muscles. Provision is thereby made to supply the muscles with the extra energy and oxygen they will need.

3) Perspiration breaks out. More evaporation will be needed to cool the body during this violent exercise.

4) Epinephrine, a hormone from the adrenal glands, is secreted into the bloodstream. This increases the sugar in the blood, providing the fuel for quick energy; it also increases the clotting ability of the blood, decreasing the amount of blood lost if the organism is wounded.

5) The electrical resistance of the skin decreases. This is the so-called *galvanic skin response*, or GSR. It is not a consequence of salty perspiration on the skin, for the decrease occurs before the perspiration reaches the surface.

6) Blood pressure increases and breathing becomes more rapid.

7) The pupils of the eyes dilate.

8) Hairs on the skin stand up, causing goose pimples. This is called *piloerection*.

EXPRESSION OF EMOTION

As in the case of motives and learning, we cannot see emotions; we must infer them from an individual's behavior. Different types of emotional expression vary somewhat according to culture and age. The roles of learning and the response of others to our emotional behavior must also be considered.

Stages of Emotional Expression. In the very young infant only various degrees of diffuse excitement can be distinguished. These may be called either positive or negative. As development proceeds, it becomes possible to differentiate distress and delight; then anger, disgust, fear, and affection become distinguishable during the first year of life.

It is thought that facial expressions accompanying positive and negative emotions early in life are the result of genetic factors. Since children born deaf and blind also show these expressions in appropriate situations, it appears plausible that maturation, rather than learning, is responsible for their development. Thus, the appearance of emotional expression may have an important innate aspect.

Recognizing Emotional Expressions.   The facial expressions associated with certain emotions have been found to be remarkably similar in several cultures. When individuals of one culture are presented with photographs of people from other cultures experiencing various emotions, they sometimes have little difficulty in correctly identifying the emotion that caused a certain facial expression.

However, such experimental results are the exception rather than the rule. Even within one culture, the expressions for particular emotions are not very standard. It has been found that much of our accuracy in judging the emotional expressions of others comes from knowing the situation which brought about the expressions. Only moderate agreement is obtained if a number of people are asked to judge what emotions caused the facial expressions shown in photographs from which all clues to the situation have been removed. It is not difficult to distinguish pleasant from unpleasant emotional expressions, but there is more disagreement when finer discriminations are called for. Apparently there is much variation from one person to another in the way emotion is expressed. (An exception to this is the startle reaction. High-speed photographs have shown that the facial expression occurring during startle is remarkably constant from one individual to the next. The eyes close, the mouth widens, the neck muscles tense, and the head ducks slightly.)

Besides facial expressions, there are other ways we can recognize emotions in others. One of these is often referred to as *body language.* Nonverbal hints can accurately communicate emotion. Some of these include hand gestures, our closeness to others when we speak with them, the amount of eye contact we make and maintain, and our tendency to touch others in the course of conversation. Body language varies widely according to culture and ethnic group.

A final characteristic of importance in emotional expression is voice quality. The loudness and tone of our voices accurately convey our feelings.

The Role of Cognition in Emotion.   The term *cognition* implies several psychological activities. These include perception, learning, memory, and judgment, to mention only a few. These activities can be summarized by the term *appraisal.* This is to say that we evaluate emotion-producing situations and behave accordingly.

This is illustrated by experiments in which different groups of subjects observed a film with highly stressful content. Each group was provided with a different pre-observation commentary on what they were about to see, thus establishing different cognitive expectations. Galvanic skin response measurements reflected differing degrees of emotional arousal for each group, depending on the nature of the commentary they heard. Information in the commentary thus influenced the appraisal of the subject's perceptions.

CAUSES OF EMOTION

Fears. One can learn to fear many things, and the causes of fear are as varied as human experience. However, several processes by which *fears* are acquired can be observed, as will be seen below.

Conditioning. A badly frightening experience may result in fear of the stimuli which were associated with that experience through a process of stimulus generalization. A child whose lack of fear of water results in his nearly being drowned may thereafter be afraid to go near water, or the beach, again. Emotional meanings become attached to objects or situations which previously did not have those meanings. Our cognitive appraisal of the rewarding or punishing aspects of emotions can become positively or negatively reinforcing. Thus emotions can be thought of not just as motives, but also as goals of our behavior.

Observation. One may learn to fear something vicariously, that is, by observing that it frightens others. A child may fear dogs because he sees that his mother does, even if the child has never had an unfortunate experience with dogs and the mother tries to avoid instilling a fear of them. We often deliberately put ourselves into situations where we might experience strong emotions vicariously. For instance, we watch daytime television dramas and read suspense-filled detective stories.

Rational Fears. We fear some things because they are in fact dangerous. It requires neither a conditioning experience nor seeing someone else display the same fear to cause the fear we feel if we recognize a rattlesnake in our path or discover that a child has just eaten a poisonous berry. We are afraid of some things because we know they can have terrible consequences. It should be emphasized that rational fear is by no means innate (see below). It is often difficult fully to separate the rational and emotional aspects of our behavior in any specific situation.

Irrational Fears. Some fears which seem perfectly rational to those who suffer from them appear irrational to those who are sure that they know better. Two examples are the medieval fear of comets, and the fear of witchcraft prevailing in some parts of the world today. Both fears would be quite rational if the consequences anticipated were actually likely to occur. Many childhood fears are irrational; they are based on superstition and misinformation as well as incomplete perceptions or the abruptness of sensory stimuli such as thunder. Most such fears disappear in the course of development.

There are other irrational fears, called *phobias*, which are very strong and persistent. These are related to the personality's defense mechanism, summarized in Chapter 10.

Innate Fears. In many species lower than man, some fears are clearly inborn. The gosling does not have to be taught to fear the shadow of the hawk. It is not clear whether man has any inborn fears, because in order to decide that a fear was innate in man, one would require convincing evidence for many individuals that they had never in their whole lives had an opportunity to acquire it.

This information is available for some chimpanzees born and reared in captivity. There are stimuli which are known never to have been experienced by them or by their fellows but which produce in them an emotional reaction. Snakes, or a model of a human head without a body, may cause considerable emotional response. This evidence shows that, in a species which in some ways behaves rather like man, fear of a thing is not always an acquired fear. It is at least possible that the same is true of man.

Anger. A frequent cause of anger or suppressed anger (also called hostility) is *frustration*, which occurs when your progress toward a goal is blocked. *Anger* and *aggression* are closely related concepts; both involve apparent restless behavior, often including feelings of tension. Both are connected with attempts to remove obstructions which block our progress toward our goals. Both mean a considerable expenditure of energy, which in itself may promote feelings of calmness and relief. This expenditure of energy is often called *catharsis*.

Anger and aggression are frequently directed at the obstructing person or object, but it is not always safe or socially appropriate to do this; as a result, we often *displace* our emotions or direct them at other persons or objects. A man having a disagreement with his boss may find it disadvantageous to display his anger. He may later direct his feelings toward his wife. On a larger scale, displaced anger and aggression may become manifested in prejudicial attitudes and behavior. Much remains to be learned about anger, because it is socially and practically difficult to arouse strong human anger under conditions favoring careful scientific observation. Ethical issues are also obvious.

Other Emotions. For the same reason that anger is difficult to study scientifically, we have few scientific data about many other emotions of great interest, particularly the positive ones. Just as negative emotions may develop from general excitability early in life through a process of stimulus generalization, so, too, may the positive emotions. *Delight, elation, affection*, and *joy* are progressively more complex emotions and make their appearance in the course of development between 3 months and 2 years of age. We know very little about the factors which elicit positive emotions or their physiological correlates.

EMOTIONS AND PERFORMANCE

It has been noted that emotions, like motives, can energize and direct behavior. Can too much emotional expression disrupt performance? A moderate amount of arousal is necessary for our performance of most tasks. But too little or too much both tend to impair our performance. As was shown in Figure 7, the difficulty of the task is important. It should also be noted that we all have different tolerances for the disruptive effects of strong emotions. Some individuals seem calm in the face of catastrophic emergencies, while others seem to "fall apart." When confronted with extreme fear-provoking situations, both humans and animals tend to "freeze."

When strong emotions are produced due to difficulties in our job, family, or personal adjustment, it is important to express these emotions constructively and to relieve feelings of tension. Until we can do so, we will probably feel that we are under a great deal of stress, and this can have definite disruptive effects on our behavior and our health. Long-lasting fear, anger, or anxiety can cause *psychosomatic illnesses*. These are physical ailments which are largely caused by psychological factors. Common examples include skin rashes, respiratory and cardio-vascular problems, ulcers, and high blood pressure, although these conditions may also arise from physical causes. It is important to recognize that not only can the efficiency of our performance suffer, but serious physical problems may accompany high arousal levels.

EMOTION AS MOTIVE

Emotions often accompany motives·and display the characteristics of goals toward which motives are directed. Emotions are also goals and sought-after states in and of themselves. The distinction between motive and emotion is somewhat blurred. The role of biological needs, acquired drives, incentives, internal stimuli, and environmental stimuli must all be considered in making such a distinction; no definitive or easy way to discriminate between the two has yet been arrived at. We know that hunger is a very strong motive, but so is the pleasurable experience of a well-prepared meal with the proper wine. Such pleasurable emotions can have definite motivating properties. Indeed, emotions can be among the most powerful motives known to man. The man who steals a car to visit his beloved, the perseverance and energy employed in the service of revenge, the injuries sustained by a mother in rescuing her children from danger—all testify to this.

In Chapter 3 we discussed the main points concerning avoidance conditioning and escape conditioning. In each of these it was noted that the acquisition of fear is an important part of learning. The ability of the emotion of fear to motivate avoidance and escape was obvious. It was also noted that behaviors followed by reinforcement are likely to be repeated, while behaviors followed by punishment are not. In these cases, pleasure derived from positive reinforcement and pain derived from punishment motivate the organism to repeat a certain behavior or not to repeat it. These basic learning principles are thus applicable to the areas of motivation and emotion; they are also related to personality growth and character disturbances, as we shall see in Chapter 10.

Chapter 7

Sensation and Perception

In this chapter we consider the senses and how they inform us about our external and internal environments. Before an organism can respond to any stimulus, its sense organs must first receive, and its brain must then process, the information supplied by that stimulus. Much of our behavior is elicited when our senses indicate to us that some action is necessary; for this reason sensory processes have relevance to many areas in psychology.

PROPERTIES COMMON TO THE SENSES

Receptors. Information about our world reaches us in the form of physical energy arriving at our sense organs, such as the patterns of light from the printed page or the airborne odor molecules from a hamburger. The information in the physical stimuli must be re-encoded into the form that the nervous system deals with, which is electrical activity in nerve fibers. Many senses are known to have a special receptor organ to accomplish this, for example, the eye or the ear. In the case of the skin senses, receptor organs have not been identified with certainty, but there must exist mechanisms by which the stimuli causing touch, temperature, or pain sensations initiate activity in the cutaneous nerves.

The receptors for each sense are connected to specific brain areas in a very orderly way, as we noted in Chapter 2. The *receptive field* of a neuron is defined by the location of stimuli that affect the neuron's activity. The arrangement of receptive fields has a map-like correspondence to the area of the brain which processes information for that sense. Receptive fields are packed closely together in those parts of sense organs where our sensitivity to stimuli is great. For instance, skin receptors are very close to each other in our lips and fingertips, and our sensitivity to tactile stimuli is very good in these areas. Correspondingly, relatively large amounts of brain tissue are devoted to processing information from such areas. Relatively small areas of the brain are devoted to areas of sense organs with a sparse density of receptors. Receptive fields frequently overlap one another, and the area which is common to two or more receptive fields is more sensitive than nonoverlapping areas. These characteristics of sense receptors are common to all the different senses.

Sensory Nerves. Information proceeding via the sensory (*afferent*) nerves to the central nervous system is encoded in the form of nerve impulses, which are brief electrical changes that are propagated along the nerve fibers. The nerve impulses representing information from different sensory modalities, such as vision or hearing or taste, show no typical difference from one another; they have the same size, shape, and duration. How, then, can we tell whether we are seeing something or tasting something? How can the brain discriminate between the neural impulses from different sense modalities?

Müller's Law of Specific Nerve Energies. The answer, Müller's law of specific nerve energies, has a name that may be misleading, since it sounds as if there were some difference in the type of nerve impulse representing each different sense. Actually, the modern form of Müller's Law is that messages from the different senses are discriminated because the nerve impulses travel over different pathways to different destinations in the brain. For instance, nerve impulses from the visual sense arrive in the visual cortex of the occipital lobe, but nerve impulses from the auditory sense arrive in the auditory cortex of the temporal lobe.

It follows that, no matter how a sense is stimulated, the resulting sensation should be appropriate to that sense, and this is in fact what happens. For instance, visual sensations can result not only from light energy striking the eye, but also from other forms of physical energy, such as a punch in the eye or electrical stimulation of the optic nerve or visual cortex. But the eye is *most* sensitive to one form of physical energy, light. It is known that for some modalities, different receptors are selectively more sensitive to quantitatively different ranges of physical energy. For instance, certain receptors in the retina of the eye are more sensitive to certain colors than to others, and one type of skin receptor is most sensitive to tactile vibrations of a very restricted frequency range.

Absolute Threshold. Every sense has an absolute threshold, that is, a certain minimum amount of physical stimulus is required before the organism can detect it. It is probably unwise to think of the absolute threshold as a definite dividing point between an amount of stimulus energy we can detect and another amount we cannot. The level of absolute threshold may vary with a number of circumstances, such as adaptation (described below), or the kind of stimulus applied. As an example of the latter, the visual threshold for red light is higher than that for yellow light. In other words, the light intensity required for you to be just able to detect a light is higher if the light is red than if it is yellow.

Differential Threshold. A certain amount of change must occur in a stimulus before one can detect that it has changed. For instance, a very weak salt solution must be doubled in concentration before you can detect that any change in saltiness has occurred. The amount of stimulus change that can be detected 50 percent of the time is the *differential threshold.* As in the case of the absolute threshold, differential thresholds vary with circumstances.

Weber's Law. E. H. Weber (1795–1878), professor of comparative anatomy and physiology at the University of Leipzig, found that the change required for a *just noticeable difference* in weight was 1/40, that for length of line 1/50, and that for auditory pitch 1/160. The important point about these ratios, called Weber fractions, is emphasized in Weber's Law: sensory discriminatory ability is not constant, but is proportional to the magnitude of the stimulus being judged.

Later research has shown that this relation does not hold precisely. If it did, the Weber fraction for a particular sensory quality would never change, whereas in fact, the Weber fraction does change, particularly at the extremes of the sensory range. As an approximate rule of thumb, however, it is still useful to remember that the amount by which a stimulus must be increased before the increase is just barely detectable tends to be proportional to the magnitude of the stimulus. For instance, suppose that you were in a room illuminated only by 100 candles, and that you could just detect the increase in illumination if one more candle were lighted. If instead there had been 200 candles in the room, two more candles would have to be lighted before you could just detect the increase in brightness.

Fechner's Law. Gustav Fechner (1801–1887), a German physician turned physicist turned philosopher, undertook to measure the magnitudes of sensations by an indirect procedure which involved the use of Weber's Law. He used the differential threshold as a measure of the just noticeable difference, or j.n.d., of sensation. Then he proposed that the subjective magnitude of a sensation could be measured by counting off the number of j.n.d.'s the sensation was above absolute threshold. From Weber's Law and from the assumption that j.n.d.'s are always equal to each other in subjective size, he derived a formula relating magnitude of subjective sensation to magnitude of the stimulus: $S = k \log R$; that is, sensation is proportional to the logarithm of the stimulus intensity (R from the German *Reiz* = stimulus; and k, a constant of proportionality that is empirically determined for a particular type of stimulus). Since Weber's Law is not exactly correct, the law Fechner derived from it cannot be either, and other objections have been raised as well.

Fechner is chiefly remembered now for his methodological contributions. In connection with his work, he employed three sets of procedures for measuring absolute and differential thresholds, procedures which are still used for these purposes today. Each of these methods concerns the ways in which experimental subjects make their judgments about the stimuli which are presented. They supply the experimenter with results he can meaningfully categorize and easily analyze. The general term used to describe such areas as the measurement of sensation in relation to some known stimulus is *psychophysics*. Fechner's historical importance is therefore that of having more than a century ago introduced into experimental psychology its first methods of measurement.

Adaptation. When there is a change in the stimulation of a sense, there results a corresponding change in sensitivity, as shown by a change in the magnitude of sensation and by a shift in absolute threshold. You demonstrate this to yourself whenever you go from a lighted room into the dark, or vice versa, and stay there long enough to notice the change in apparent brightness as you adapt. In all the senses, adaptation depends on a stimulus' having occurred over some length of time, and it consists of a decrease in the sensitivity of receptors. Often, adaptation causes only a change in sensation level and absolute threshold, but sometimes it results in complete disappearance of sensation, as when you no longer feel the pencil tucked above your ear, not because you come to disregard it, but because touch sensitivity has decreased. Adaptation may be measured with psychophysical procedures, and the neural activity in sensory nerves can be recorded by employing the techniques outlined in Chapter 2.

Masking. Our sense organs continually receive physical energy of different quality and quantity. Because of this, it is often difficult to sort out and attend to a single, "pure" stimulus. When a stimulus of a large magnitude makes it difficult or impossible for us to perceive one of smaller magnitude, we say that the former "masks" the latter. Low, loud tones mask high-pitched ones. Certain odors mask others, as is apparent in our deodorant-oriented society. Eating certain foods will mask more subtle flavors, as the wine steward readily knows. In masking, the presence of one stimulus decreases our sensitivity to another.

PERCEPTUAL ORGANIZATION

In the early part of this century, the Gestalt psychologists were very interested in why things appear as they do. The German word *Gestalt* means "form" or "configuration." The Gestalt psychologists described several principles influencing organization in perception. They thought that stimulus components are not processed separately from one another, that the brain does not recognize individual components and then combine them to construct a meaningful whole. Rather, they felt that the brain is organized in such a way that the whole is different from the mere sum of its parts. The relationship between many stimuli is important. The Gestalt theory dealt primarily with visual perception, although the principles summarized below have analogues in other senses.

Figure and Ground. Patterns are perceived as a foreground against a background, in which the figure (the foreground) stands out from the ground (background). Figure 9 is a reversible configuration, in which either the dark portion or the white portion can be perceived as the figure. In listening to a Bach fugue, we are able to recognize a background melody with a different melody superimposed on it. The ability to discriminate figure from ground appears to be one of the earliest perceptual skills to develop in infants.

Patterning. We all have a need to organize what we perceive; in this way stimuli become meaningful to us. By organizing, we construct wholes from many stimuli, the whole being more important than the sum of its parts according to the Gestalt view. There are several basic facts that are known about the individual's tendencies in perceiving patterns of various types.

a) *Similarity.* Similar items tend to be seen as belonging together. (Figure 10a.)

b) *Closure.* Incomplete figures tend to be perceived as complete. (Figure 10b.)

c) *Proximity.* Elements which are close together tend to be perceived as belonging together. (Figure 10c.)

d) *Good Continuation.* When part of the pattern can be perceived either as changing suddenly or as continuing smoothly,

Fig. 9. Reversible Configuration

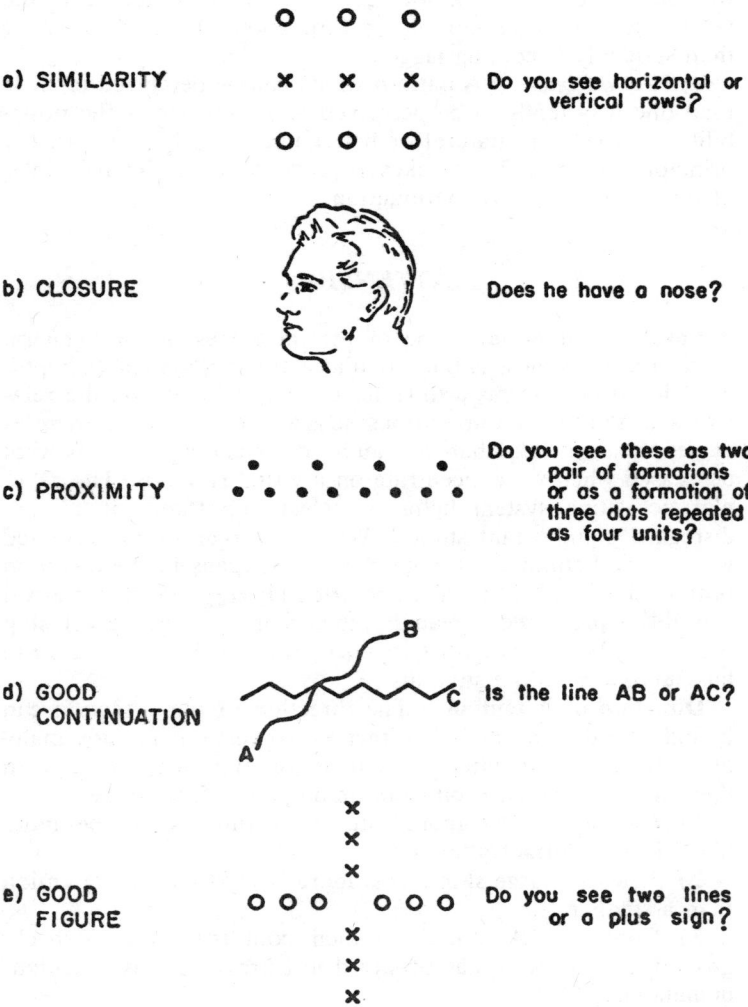

a) SIMILARITY   Do you see horizontal or vertical rows?

b) CLOSURE   Does he have a nose?

c) PROXIMITY   Do you see these as two pair of formations or as a formation of three dots repeated as four units?

d) GOOD CONTINUATION   Is the line AB or AC?

e) GOOD FIGURE   Do you see two lines or a plus sign?

Fig. 10. Patterning

we tend to perceive a smooth continuation. In Figure 10d, the wavy line is seen as continuing throughout the pattern rather than suddenly becoming jagged.

e) *Good Figure.*   A pattern which can be perceived in more than one way tends to be perceived as whichever of the possibilities is the more natural or better figure. In Figure 10e, the principle of good figure takes precedence over the principles of similarity and good continuation.

ATTENTION

Level of Attention.   One of the influences on our general level of attentiveness is the reticular activating system (Chapter 2). This system seems also to have some influence on the relative sensitivities of our various senses. For example, there is evidence suggesting that our auditory sensitivity is somewhat decreased when we concentrate on a visual stimulus. The reticular activating system helps us select important stimuli and disregard unimportant stimuli. When an organism is presented with a novel stimulus, it aligns its sense organs in the direction of that stimulus. This is called an *orienting response.* If the novel stimulus is presented repeatedly, the orienting response will stop occurring. When this has happened, we say that the organism has *habituated* to the stimulus.

Direction of Attention.   The direction of our attention can be influenced by a number of factors. Advertisers employ many of these factors in attempting to direct our attention toward their advertisements. Prominent among these factors are:

1) *Intensity.*   The more intense a stimulus is, the more likely it is to attract attention.

2) *Size.*   A large stimulus is more likely to attract attention than a smaller one.

3) *Contrast.*   A stimulus which contrasts with its background, or with what has occurred just previously, is attention-demanding.

4) *Movement.*   A moving stimulus is more attention-getting than a stationary one.

5) *Repetition.*   A stimulus has a better chance of catching our attention if it is repeated.

6) *Motives.*   A stimulus is attention-demanding if it appeals to our likes, dislikes, interests, fears, deprivations, and so on.

VISION

Physical Stimuli. The modern physical concept of light is quite abstract. However, for many purposes including ours, light can be thought of as being that electromagnetic radiation which we can see. We can think of electromagnetic radiations as traveling through space in either waves or particles.

One specification of light is then in terms of its *wavelength*—that is, the distance from the peak of one wave to that of the next. The range of wavelengths which the human eye sees as light varies with stimulating conditions, but the range usually given is from 380 nanometers to 760 nanometers. (A *nanometer* is one-billionth of a meter.)

Light is also specified in terms of its intensity. There are several different units for specifying light intensity. Light intensity is a function of wave amplitude.

The Eye As Receptor. The principal parts of the eye are shown in cross-section in Figure 11.

Cornea. In addition to serving as protection for the iris, the cornea is part of the lens system of the eye. About two-thirds of the refractive power in the eye is due to the cornea. It is made of protein.

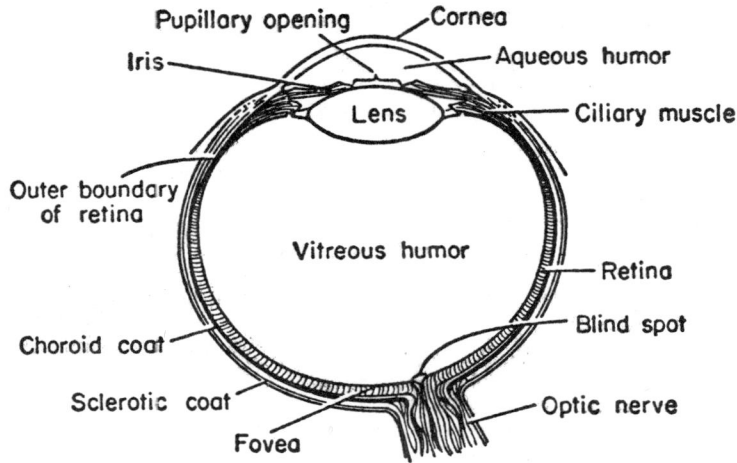

Fig. 11. The Eye

Iris. The iris is the part of the eye which we refer to when we say somebody has blue eyes or brown eyes. The iris has two sets of very small muscles which open and constrict the pupil and thereby help control the amount of light entering the eye as illumination changes. Pupillary changes can effect only a bit more than a sixteen-fold change in the amount of light entering the eye, and the major part of adaptation to differing light conditions takes place in sensory cells and neurons. The opening of the pupil ranges from 2 millimeters to 8 millimeters. Light passing through the center of the pupil is more effective in producing images than light entering the eye near the margin of the pupil.

Lens. The lens is the adjustable element in the lens system of the eye. By becoming thicker or thinner, it adjusts focus for the distance of the stimulus viewed.

Retina. The retina is the layer containing the rods and the cones, which are the sensory cells responsible for transforming light energy into the electrical changes that carry visual information in the nervous system. Each retina has about 6½ million cones and 125 million rods, and chemical differences are known to exist in the two types of receptor. Most of the retina, except for the fovea and the blind spot described below, contains both rods and cones. Other types of cells are also found in the retina, and the interactions among these cells are important in the visual process whereby images are formed.

Cones. In daylight levels of illumination, the sensory cells upon which vision depends are the cones, which are less sensitive to light than the rods. It is also the cones which are responsible for discrimination among hues. Functionally different types of cones are selectively responsive to different parts of the light spectrum.

Rods. At very dim levels of illumination, the cones are not sensitive enough to respond, and then the rods are the sensory cells which are responsible for vision. When one has become completely adapted to total darkness, he can detect an amount of light which is not so far from the minimum amount of light which can physically exist according to the quantum theory of light.

One cannot distinguish among different hues when only the rods are stimulated. The world looks like a black-and-white photograph.

Fovea. The fovea is a small pit which, unlike the rest of the retina, contains only cones. It is the part of the retina on which the image of the exact point at which one is looking is located. It is the part of the retina capable of the greatest visual acuity (the greatest ability to see fine details). The fovea is smaller than 1 square millimeter and has over 50,000 cones.

There are two results of these characteristics of the fovea. First, in daylight illumination one sees most clearly the point at which he is looking, because it is that part of the visual image which falls on the fovea. Visual acuity is surprisingly poor for the image at a distance from the fovea. Second, in very dim illumination, the exact point at which one is looking is not seen at all, because that part of the image falls on the fovea, which, as we have mentioned, has no rods. For this reason, those who are looking for a faint star or navigation light are well advised to look slightly to the side of the place where the light should appear, so that its image will fall on rods.

Blind Spot. At the point where the nerve fibers from the sensory cells join together as the optic nerve and leave the eye, there are no receptor cells. The small part of the visual image which falls on this part of the retina is not seen. Because the blind spots of the two eyes are not located at corresponding parts of the two visual images, the blind spot ordinarily is unnoticed. Even when only one eye is being used, the part of the image affected is so small that there is seldom any practical effect.

One can demonstrate the blind spot for himself by marking two heavy dots about two inches apart on a sheet of paper. Gaze with the left eye at the dot on the right, or with the right eye at the dot on the left, while closing the other eye. When the paper has been brought to within five or six inches of the eye, the dot not being looked at directly will disappear, because its image falls on the blind spot.

Optic Nerve. Each optic nerve has about one million fibers which conduct nerve impulses to the brain.

Defects in Focusing. There are four basic types of defective focusing, each of which we will discuss below.

"Near-sightedness" (myopia). Near-sightedness does not mean that the individual with this defect has better than normal vision at near distances, but only that he cannot focus on distant objects. This is usually because his eyeball is too long, so that

the lens cannot flatten enough to bring the images of distant objects into clear focus on the retina. Instead, they are focused slightly in front of it.

"Far-sightedness" (hyperopia, hypermetropia).   Far-sightedness does not mean that the individual has better than normal vision for objects at a greater distance, but only that he cannot focus on objects close by. This is usually because his eyeball is too short, so that the lens cannot thicken enough to bring the image of near objects into clear focus. The image is instead formed slightly behind the retina.

Astigmatism.   If the cornea's curvature is not the same in all directions, then the cornea is a thicker lens in some directions than in others. Consequently, even when some parts of the scene are in clear focus, other parts will be out of focus.

Presbyopia.   As we grow older, there is a weakening of the muscles which control the lens of the eye. As a result, the nearest point on which we can focus clearly becomes farther away. Eventually we may find that we have to hold a book uncomfortably far away in order to read it.

Correction of Focusing Defects.   The foregoing focusing defects are corrected by adding suitable supplementary lenses, in the form of eyeglasses or contact lenses, to the lens system of the eye.

Stimulus and Sensation in Vision.

Color.   In everyday language, when we say "color," we mean hue. A color actually presents three nearly independent sensory qualities: hue, brightness, and saturation.

HUE.   Hue is the characteristic of a color perception that determines whether it is red, yellow, green, blue, and so on. The hue we perceive when looking at a pure light depends on the wavelength of the light. The hues in order from the long-wave to the short-wave end of the spectrum are red, orange, yellow, green, blue, violet.

BRIGHTNESS.   Brightness is the subjective attribute of a color that describes where it would fall on a scale from bright to dim. The corresponding physical attribute is intensity, a more intense light appearing brighter. Brightness is dependent upon the amount of energy coming from a light source. Large-amplitude light waves will be perceived as bright.

SATURATION.   Saturation refers to the purity of a color. Highly saturated colors do not have much grey in them; they are vivid. Unsaturated colors have more grey in them and appear pale or washed-out. When many different wavelengths are mixed together, the resulting color will not be very saturated; when only a few are mixed together the resulting color will be very saturated.

In everyday life we are used to discriminating among hues and brightnesses, but not among saturations, so it may help if you visualize an experiment in which saturation is varied while hue and brightness are held constant. Imagine that you have a can of green paint and a can of grey paint, both of exactly the same brightness so that any mixtures of the two do not result in a brightness change. Now, while stirring the grey paint, slowly add green paint, drop by drop, until you can detect a green tinge to the grey paint. You have now produced a very desaturated green. As you continue, producing greens which are less and less washed-out in appearance, you are increasing the saturation of the green mixture. The hue remains green, brightness remains unchanged, only the saturation is changing.

If you had wanted to produce only a slight desaturation of the green, you would have proceeded in the reverse direction. You would have added a small amount of grey paint to that in the green can.

Table of Stimulus and Sensation in Vision. The foregoing relations between stimulus and sensation are summarized as follows:

Physical Stimulus	*Sensation*
Wavelength of light	Hue
Intensity of light	Brightness
Purity of light	Saturation

Additive Color Mixing. The principles of additive color mixing describe the hues seen when light of more than one wavelength stimulates the eye. One way of producing an additive color mixture is to shine two lights of different wavelengths on the same white paper.

The results of additive color mixture are in general not the same as those of subtractive color mixture with which we are familiar from mixing paints. (Color filters also operate subtractively.) Each paint subtracts some degree of various wavelengths from the light falling on it and reflects the remainder to our eyes. When paints are mixed (or color filters are superimposed) the hue seen depends on the intensities of the wavelengths remaining after the resulting double subtraction. On the other hand in additive color mixtures, in which light of more than one wavelength stimulates the eye, the hue resulting from the mixture of wavelengths is a result of the properties of the color vision system of the eye. As an example of the different results of the two kinds of mixture, a subtractive mixture resulting from mixing blue and yellow paints typically appears green, but an additive mixture of the proper amounts of blue and yellow light appears white. Color television produces its effects by additive color mixture.

Additive Mixture of Complementary Colors. A pair of colors are complementary to each other if they lie directly opposite each other on the color wheel (Figure 12). A pair of complementary colors mixed in the proper proportion appear grey or white, depending on brightness. If they are mixed in other proportions, one sees a desaturated version of one of the two hues.

Additive Mixture of Non-Complementary Colors. Non-complementary colors do not lie directly opposite each other on the rim of the color wheel. When mixed, they result in a color between them, in hue and in saturation.

Color Zones. Hues are not always seen all the way out to the edge of the visual field. Both visual acuity and color vision tend to diminish in the peripheral parts of the retina; this is more noticeable the further the image is from the fovea. Suppose that you have a friend select a quarter-inch square of

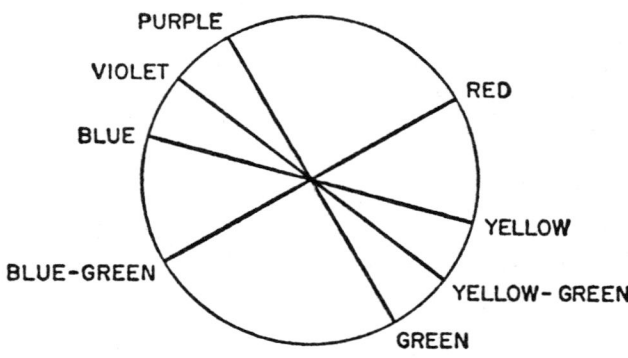

Fig. 12. Color Wheel

colored paper without your knowing what hue it is. Have him start at the very edge of your visual field and slowly move the paper toward the center of the field. You will probably be able to see the square for some little time before you can correctly identify its hue. A systematic exploration of your visual field would show that there is a color zone inside which you can see this hue, but outside of which it either looks like a different color or seems to have no color at all. In general, the color zones for red and green are smaller than those for yellow and blue.

If the stimuli are larger or more intense, then the color zones will be larger, and may extend all the way to the edge of the visual field. Thus the existence of color zones does not mean that your peripheral visual field has no color vision, but only that it is less sensitive. Moving from the fovea to the peripheral retina, one finds fewer and fewer cones and more and more rods.

Color "Blindness." Color blindness is in most cases an inaccurate term, for the "color-blind individual is not truly blind to colors, but confuses certain ones with each other. Only in the very rare cases of total color blindness does the world look like a black-and-white photograph to the individual. In these rare cases, it is clear that only the rods are functioning. Only about 25 people out of a million are totally color blind.

There are several theories of color vision, but none is totally satisfactory. Certain aspects of each theory seem to work well in explaining certain phenomena of color perception. Thus, there is no completely satisfactory explanation for the various types of color blindness. No cure is known. Certain genetic defects, poisons, and nutritional insufficiencies can cause one form or another of color blindness.

Since there are functionally different types of cones, the absence or malfunction of one type of cone could possibly be responsible for color blindness. Each type of cone contains a special chemical or *photopigment* that is specifically sensitive to light of a certain range of wavelengths. If such a photopigment is missing, the brain cannot receive any color information from that group of cones.

Red-Green Color Blindness. There is more than one type of red-green blindness, but all have in common the fact that the individuals concerned confuse certain reds and greens with each other. From the reports of a few individuals who have had this defect in one eye, but normal color vision in the other, we know that to the red-green color-blind eye, reds and greens look the way that desaturated yellows do to the person with normal color vision. Red-green color blindness is genetically determined, and is sex-linked, occurring more often in males than in females.

Yellow-Blue Color Blindness.   In this comparatively rare form of color blindness, yellows and blues are confused with each other.

Color "Weakness."   Some individuals, while not color blind, need to mix an unusually large amount of one color with another to produce a third color. For instance, someone with a color weakness for blue would need to add much more blue to yellow to produce green than an individual without the color weakness.

Depth Perception.   Our visual field projects an image on the retina of the eye which is upside down and reversed. There is a correspondence, even though it is a reverse one, between right-left and up-down location of objects in our visual field and the parts of the retina on which the corresponding images fall. For instance, the image of something to the left of our line of regard falls on the right side of the retina, the image of something above our line of regard falls on the lower part of the retina. This is a clue sufficient for us to locate an object visually in two dimensions, horizontally and vertically. But how can we detect differences in the third dimension, distance away from us? What are the clues that help us in depth perception?

Binocular Vision.   When we are using both eyes, the most important clue to distance is retinal disparity.

RETINAL DISPARITY.   There is a disparity, a difference, between the retinal images in the right and left eyes. Since the two eyes are spatially separated, the right eye sees a little farther around the right side of an object, and the left eye sees a little farther around the left side, so there is a slight difference in the two retinal images of that object. The closer the object is to the viewer, the more retinal disparity there is, and this provides a clue to the distance of the object.

This is the principle employed in three-dimensional movies and photographs. Pictures are taken through two lenses, one to the right of the other, producing a disparity in the images on the film. By one or another optical means, the photograph taken through the lens on the right is presented to the viewer's right eye, and the photograph taken through the lens on the left is presented to the viewer's left eye, producing a retinal disparity which results in the perception of depth.

Monocular Vision. Many clues to distance remain, even if binocular clues are eliminated, for instance by closing one eye. These monocular clues, listed below, also help binocular depth perception, and some are responsible for the appearance of depth in paintings and photographs.

ACCOMMODATION. At comparatively near distances, the curvature of the lens of the eye which is required in order to provide a clearly focused retinal image is a clue to the distance of the object focused on. The ciliary muscles change the convexity of the lens and there are believed to be sensory receptors which report the activity of these muscles.

RELATIVE SIZE. The apparent relative size of objects of known size provides a clue to their distance.

SUPERPOSITION. If one object cuts off part or all of the view of another, the first object is perceived as being in front of the second.

SHADING. In ordinary illumination, three-dimensional objects are shaded more on one side than another, which helps to give a three-dimensional appearance.

CLARITY. Details of far distant objects, such as mountains, are less clearly seen because of scattering of light by dust particles and water vapor in the atmosphere. The clarity of the atmosphere at higher altitudes has misled more than one hiker into setting out toward a mountain that was much farther away than it seemed to be, an example showing that clues in depth perception are sometimes misleading.

TEXTURE GRADIENTS. Many ordinary surfaces such as roads or patches of soil have a texture which appears to grow smaller as its distance increases, providing another clue to distance.

RELATIVE MOVEMENT. Objects, such as trains and airplanes, whose velocity is roughly known, provide clues to their distances by the fact that they appear to move more slowly when farther away.

When an observer is himself moving, nearby objects appear to move more rapidly across the visual field than distant ones do.

Experience. There is some evidence that one learns to use shading as a clue in three-dimensional depth perception. On the other hand, the ability to perceive depth on the basis of relative movement apparently requires no practice for its development.

Perceptual Constancies. We tend to see an object as being constant in its characteristics, even when there are considerable differences in the actual stimulation it provides the receptor from time to time.

Shape Constancy. An object tends to be seen as having the same shape, in spite of changes in the angle from which it is viewed. For instance, a dinner plate may at one time project a circular image on the retina, while if viewed at another angle its retinal image is an ellipse. We do not perceive the plate as correspondingly changing its shape.

Size Constancy. The size of the retinal image of an object varies according to the distance of the object. We do not perceive the object as correspondingly changing its size. For instance, when you move a book to twice the distance from your eyes, it does not appear to shrink to half its former size.

Brightness Constancy. The change in the amount of illumination falling on an object changes the amount of light that it reflects to our eyes; but we tend to see the object remaining the same brightness, rather than changing brightness in accord with the change in intensity of retinal stimulation. When thunder clouds cover a previously clear sky, we do not perceive white shirts as turning to a dark grey.

Hue Constancy. In spite of moderate changes in the color balance of the prevailing illumination, we ordinarily do not see corresponding changes in the hues of objects. The white shirt does not appear to have turned red at sunset, nor to turn yellow when one goes indoors into tungsten illumination.

Location Constancy. When one turns his head, he does not perceive the world as moving, although its image moves on his retina. (The world can appear to move when its retinal image moves. You can demonstrate this to yourself by pressing very gently on the side of your eyelid.)

After-Images. If an image is allowed to fall on the retina for only a very brief period of time, the sensation will outlast the stimulus for a short period of time. These *after-images* can be seen after the abrupt termination of stimulation if one then gazes at a homogeneous visual field. They demonstrate that the consequences of visual stimulation outlast the stimulation.

As an after-image fades away, its form may change somewhat. These changes tend to follow the principles of patterning described above as suggested by the Gestalt psychologists. Fading images become more rounded and less disconnected, and incomplete images tend to be perceived as complete.

Positive After-Images. Positive after-images resemble the stimulus in hue and brightness. They are more easily seen after a short intense stimulation before which one was dark-adapted. For a demonstration, watch a light bulb turned on and off in a dark room. It is a positive after-image which disrupts our visual acuity temporarily when we view the high-beam headlights of an oncoming car.

Negative After-Images. In negative after-images, brightnesses are reversed and hues are complementary. They are usually seen by first gazing fixedly at a stimulus for half a minute or so, then transferring one's gaze to a grey or white background.

The Brain and Vision. Many studies have been done in which the neural activity of different areas of the brain dealing with vision has been recorded. These sites include the thalamus and the visual area of the cortex. In both areas there are nerve cells that respond preferentially to certain hues. Also, nerve cells in the visual cortex have been found to respond vigorously when straight lines of some orientations are presented to the eye and to become unresponsive when straight lines of other orientations are presented. It is as though cells in the visual cortex have a preferred stimulus.

HEARING

Physical Stimuli. Waves of alternate compression and rarefaction traveling through some elastic medium such as air, water, or steel are called *sound* if their wavelengths lie in the range which we can hear. These waves travel at different speeds in different mediums.

Measuring Sound. The principal measures of sound are *frequency* and *intensity.*

FREQUENCY. For various reasons a sound is usually described not in terms of its wavelength, but in terms of its frequency. (Frequency is reciprocally related to wavelength.) The frequency of a sound refers to the number of complete cycles (Figure 13) which pass a given point in one second. For instance, it is usually said that the range of sound frequencies audible to the normal young human ear is from 20 cycles per second to 20,000 cycles per second. The unit of physical measurement for frequency is the *hertz* (abbreviated *hz*), named

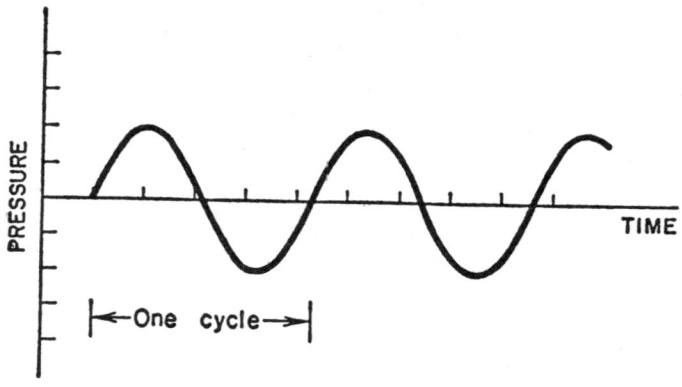

Fig. 13. Sound Waves

after the German physicist Heinrich F. Hertz (1857–1894). Instead of saying "20 cycles per second," we say "20 hz."

Actually, the two extremes of this range are different in nature. Frequencies above approximately 20,000 per second are inaudible to the human; frequencies near 20 hz. are audible to the human, but no longer sound like tones.

INTENSITY (AMPLITUDE). The unit of sound intensity is the *decibel*. The range of human hearing at its best is in the neighborhood of 120 decibels. The decibel is logarithmically related to sound wave amplitude, and this figure represents a range of amplitudes of a million to one with which the human ear can deal.

Complexity. Much everyday sound is composed of more than one frequency; pure tones are rare in our daily lives.

OVERTONES (HARMONICS). Many musical instruments, and some other sound sources, produce sounds containing several frequencies which are simple multiples of the lowest frequency. For instance, a musical instrument sounding a tone of 440 hz. may also be producing frequencies of 880 hz., 1760 hz., 2640 hz., and so on. The lowest frequency is called the *fundamental* frequency (synonym: first *harmonic*), and the succeedingly higher frequencies are called the first, second, third, fourth, etc., harmonics or *overtones*.

A different kind of musical instrument playing the same note might also produce sound containing these same frequencies. In the second sound the relative intensities of the various frequencies would be different than in the first sound, which is why you can distinguish between two different instruments such as a saxophone and a piano playing the same note. (See "Timbre" below.)

NOISE. As sound waves become less repetitive in wave form and amplitude, and more irregular, they sound less like tones and more like noise. Noise is a random collection of various frequencies with differing amplitudes. The characteristics of speech are in some ways rather like tones and in some ways rather like noise.

The Ear as Receptor. The principal parts of the ear are shown in cross-section in Figure 14.

External Auditory Canal. The auditory canal provides a channel through which sound waves are funneled toward the eardrum.

Eardrum. The eardrum is a membrane which is set into vibration by the arriving sound waves. It is also called the *tympanic membrane.*

Ossicles (Hammer, Anvil, and Stirrup). These three tiny bones transmit the sound vibrations to the oval window of the

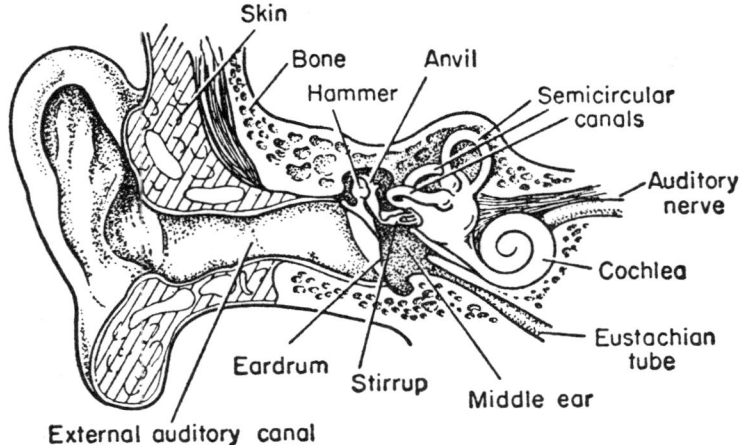

Fig. 14. The Ear

cochlea. They constitute a lever system which increases the pressure variations transmitted to the oval window, thus aiding the transfer of these vibrations to the fluid within the cochlea.

Cochlea.   The fluid-filled cochlea contains the mechanisms which convert sound vibrations into electrical impulses in auditory nerve fibers.

Basilar Membrane.   Figure 15 is a cross-section of one turn of the cochlea showing the basilar membrane, which follows the spirals of the cochlea. The pressure variations at the oval window result in traveling waves of vibration in the basilar membrane. A change in sound frequency changes the location of maximum vibration on the basilar membrane.

Organ of Corti.   The organ of Corti contains the specialized endings of the auditory nerve fibers which are stimulated by movement of the basilar membrane.

Auditory Nerve.   Nerve fibers of the auditory nerve conduct nerve impulses to the brain.

Stimulus and Sensation in Hearing.

Properties of Tones.   The three principal characteristics of a tone or pure sound are *pitch, loudness,* and *timbre.*

PITCH.   Pitch is the characteristic of a tone that we are referring to when we describe a flute as high-pitched, a bassoon as low-pitched. The pitch we hear depends primarily on the frequency of the tone. The range of fundamental frequencies of

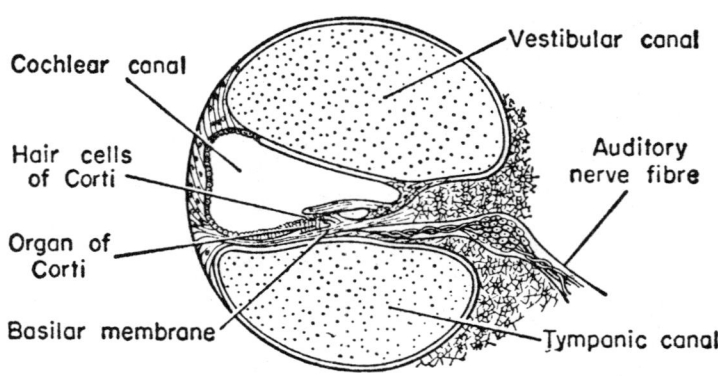

Fig. 15.   Cross-section of One Turn of the Cochlea

a grand piano may be from less than 30 hz. to more than 4000 hz.

LOUDNESS. The subjective strength of a sound is described as loudness, and depends principally on the amplitude of the sound waves. A whisper may have an intensity of 20 decibels, a loud clap of thunder, 120 decibels.

TIMBRE. Timbre is the characteristic of a sound which enables us to identify the sound source. For instance, the musical note of middle C has the same fundamental sound frequency whether it is produced by a soprano or by a trumpet, but each of these two sound sources has its own characteristic sound, or timbre, which enables us to tell which of them produced the tone.

Differences in timbre result from differences in the relative intensities of the various overtones (harmonics) produced by different sound sources.

Table of Stimulus and Sensation in Hearing. The foregoing relations between stimulus and sensation are summarized as follows:

Physical Stimulus	*Sensation*
Frequency of sound waves	Pitch
Amplitude of sound waves	Loudness
Relative strength of overtones (harmonics)	Timbre

Sound Mixtures. The auditory system, unlike the visual system, is very good at analyzing mixtures into their components. Light of two different wavelengths is seen as a single color; sound of two different wavelengths (frequencies) is usually heard as two different tones. The listener can distinguish the different instruments while the whole band plays.

BEATS. Because the ear is not a perfect analyzer, sound frequencies close together are heard as a single note, cylically varying in loudness at the frequency of the difference between the two sound frequencies. For example, when tones of 440 hz. and 437 hz. are sounded together, you hear a tone of intermediate pitch passing through three cycles of loudness per second.

SPEECH SOUNDS. Speech sounds contain a great number of different frequencies, but the major part of the sound energy is concentrated below 2000 hz. However, for the understanding of speech, the frequencies above 2000 hz. are as important as those below. There are two reasons for this. First it is easier to distinguish among the vowels if we can hear the overtones (harmonics), many of which are at higher frequencies. Second, consonants, which are important in distinguishing among words, are full of higher-frequency components.

Defects in Hearing. There are two general classes of deafness. One is called "conduction deafness," the other is called "nerve deafness."

Conduction Deafness. Conduction deafness results from mechanical interference with the transmission of sound to the cochlea. For instance, it can be produced by wax in the ear, or fluid in the middle ear, or a bony buildup causing the stirrup bone to "stick" at the oval window. The consequence is usually an increase in absolute threshold which is comparatively uniform for all frequencies.

This kind of deafness can sometimes be alleviated by surgical treatment or circumvented by the use of a hearing aid.

Nerve Deafness. Nerve deafness results from damage to the auditory nerve, or to the receptor system in the cochlea. The damage may result from disease, injurious levels of sound, or from degeneration due to aging. There is likely to be either a proportionately greater rise in absolute threshold at the higher frequencies, or a rise over a rather restricted range of frequencies.

Since this kind of deafness results from damage to nerve fibers or to receptors, which do not regenerate, it cannot be cured. In some cases the impairment may be diminished through the use of a hearing aid, however.

Auditory Space Perception. Solely through the use of our ears, we can discriminate the direction from which sound comes, and can tell whether it is nearby or far away. How do we do it?

Direction of Sound. If the sound source is somewhere on a line straight ahead of you, the distances from your two ears to it are the same, and the sound arrives at both ears at the same time. If the sound source is to the left or to the right of this line, the sound waves have to travel farther in reaching one of your ears than they do in reaching the other, and so there is a difference in time of arrival of the sound at the two ears. This small time difference, which may be less than 1/10,000th of a second, results in your hearing the sound as displaced to the right or to the left, to a degree corresponding to the amount of the time difference.

The second clue to the direction of the sound source comes from the fact that the sound waves have to bend around your head to enter your ear, and higher-frequency sound waves do not do this as well as those of lower frequency do, so they are not as loud on the side of your head away from the sound source.

Differences in time of arrival at the two ears tend to be more effective clues at frequencies below the region of 3000 hz. Above this region, intensity differences tend to be more effective clues.

From the foregoing analysis, it follows that auditory discrimination of right and left directions should be very good, while it should be very poor for front-back and up-down differences. This is in fact the case, though you can improve these discriminations somewhat by moving your head as you listen.

Distance of Sound. The distance of sound sources with which we have had experience can be judged on the basis of the loudness of the sound. In addition, there is often a change in timbre as the distance of the sound sources increases, because the higher-frequency components tend to become weakened more than the lower as they travel.

THE CUTANEOUS SENSES

Physical Stimuli. The cutaneous senses respond to mechanical deformation, temperature, and to sufficiently intense stimuli of nearly any sort. In contrast to the stimuli for the eye and the ear, the stimuli for the cutaneous senses usually come from sources near the skin or on it.

The Skin As Receptor. The skin is the body's most extensive sense organ, covering its entire surface. It has *punctate sensitivity*, that is, it has some points or spots on it which are more sensitive than others. Some points are more sensitive to mechanical energy, some to cold, some to heat, and some to pain. The kind of "spot" which occurs most frequently on the body is that for pain, then comes touch, then cold, and finally heat.

Within the tissues under these spots, one finds various sorts of nerve endings. Most common are the free nerve endings, fine filaments which are the ends of cutaneous nerve fibers. In addition, there are nerve endings with associated non-neural tissue, often in the form of tiny capsules of various shapes and sizes enclosing nerve endings both on the surface of the skin and beneath it. Many decades ago it was proposed that these different nerve endings might be different receptor organs for the cutaneous senses. It is now known that there are some body areas capable of all the usual cutaneous sensations although these areas are supplied with only free nerve endings. It is therefore clear that the encapsulated structures sometimes observed are not necessary to the production of cutaneous sensation, although in some cases they modify the duration of the sensation.

Stimulus and Sensation in the Cutaneous Senses.

Touch, Pressure. Sensations of touch or pressure are aroused when mechanical energy causes a gradient of tension in the skin. The force, area, mass, and acceleration of the stimulus are all important.

Temperature. Sensations of warmth or of cold are aroused by stimuli which sufficiently raise or lower the temperature of the skin. This can be achieved by sources which touch the skin and change its temperature or by sources some distance from the skin surface that do so. Skin receptors have been found that are selectively responsive to warmth, and others that are selectively sensitive to cooling. The rate of temperature change and the spatial extent of skin over which it takes place are also important features of temperature sensitivity.

PHYSIOLOGICAL ZERO. There is a small range of temperature (differing in size for different parts of the body) which arouses sensations neither of warmth nor of cold. This range, called physiological zero, usually includes the skin temperature and a narrow range of temperatures on either side of it, called the *neutral zone.* When the skin is stimulated with heat, both boundaries of this range move in the same direction. That is, the absolute thresholds for both warmth and cold are now found at higher temperatures than they were before heat stimulation.

Pain. Sufficiently strong stimulation with almost any kind of physical energy results in sensations of pain. Such stimuli include infra-red radiation, electrical current, mechanical deformation, and chemical stimuli. Cutaneous pain is usually considered to be a phenomenon different from "deep" pain, which is, for example, associated with muscular aches. Also, tissue damage and the occurrence of pain do not always go hand in hand.

There are a very few, rare individuals born with a congenital insensitivity to stimuli interpreted as painful by the majority of the population. These people having unusually high thresholds to painful stimuli are sometimes called *pain-blind*.

TASTE

Physical Stimuli. To reach the taste receptors on the tongue, a substance must be soluble in saliva. However, not all substances which are soluble in saliva have a taste.

Taste stimuli are specified in terms of their chemical composition and their concentration. Other characteristics of stimuli which influence our perception of taste include odor, texture, and temperature.

The Tongue as Receptor. There are tiny pits called taste buds on the tongue and on some nearby areas. Sometimes several of these taste buds are bunched together in a structure called a *papilla*. Within each bud is a group of taste receptor cells which are the ends of the nerve fibers that conduct to the brain the nerve impulses resulting from taste stimulation. One theory of taste reception holds that molecules of food substances fit into very tiny holes in the receptor cells and thereby initiate these nerve impulses.

Taste "Blindness." There are marked differences among people in their absolute thresholds for certain taste stimuli. There has been considerable investigation of taste "blindness," with much attention having been given to a substance known as PTC (phenylthiocarbamide, phenylthiourea). Taste "blindness" turns out to be a misleading name, since it sounds as if it were an all-or-none matter, whereas there is actually a wide range of sensitivities to the bitter taste of PTC. However, people tend to fall into two groups with respect to their absolute thresholds for PTC, one of higher sensitivities, and one of lower sensitivities for whom concentrations of PTC must be around a thousand times greater before it can be detected. There is evidence from population genetics to suggest that these differences are hereditary.

Stimulus and Sensation in Tasting. The four basic taste qualities we can distinguish are sour, salty, bitter, and sweet. The other qualities we ordinarily think of in connection with the tastes of things result from stimulation of the cutaneous senses in the mouth and often from stimulation of the sense of smell. Responsiveness to these categories of stimuli is believed to exist at birth.

SOUR. The degree to which something tastes sour depends upon the concentration of hydrogen ions it causes at the receptors.

SALTY. Common table salt, and many but not all of the other chemical compounds classed as salts, taste salty. Equal concentrations of two different salts may cause very different perceptions of the degree of saltiness.

BITTER. Many classes of chemical compounds taste bitter, the best known being the alkaloids. No chemical or physical characteristics common to all bitter compounds has been discovered.

SWEET. No chemical or physical characteristic common to all sweet compounds has yet been discovered. Most but not all sweet-tasting substances are organic compounds.

Adaptation. Prolonged exposure to taste stimuli on the surface of the tongue gradually results in a loss of sensitivity (raised threshold) to the substance. Sometimes recovery of sensitivity takes up to 30 minutes.

SMELL

Physical Stimuli. In order to reach the odor receptors, the physical stimulus must be volatile, that is, capable of evaporating or vaporizing. However, not all volatile substances have an odor. Odorous substances are usually specified in terms of their chemical composition and their concentration in the air. Marine animals receive odors dissolved in water.

The Olfactory Rods as Receptors. High at the top of the nasal passages within the head is a sheet of tissue called the *olfactory epithelium (olfactory mucosa)*. In this tissue are millions of receptor cells, the *olfactory rods*, which are endings of the olfactory nerve fibers. These olfactory rods have several fine, finger-like extensions which are believed to pick up airborne molecules and initiate a nerve impulse which is conveyed to the brain. Other olfactory receptors are thought to exist in the nasal passages and the pharynx.

Stimulus and Sensation in Olfaction. Though various theories have been proposed, there are for the sense of smell no generally accepted basic qualitative dimensions, analogous for instance to sour, salty, sweet, and bitter in the sense of taste. Nevertheless, attempts at such a classification have been made.

Similarly, there have as yet been found no broad generalizations relating chemical composition to kind of odor, though there are some principles of limited generality. One contemporary view holds that the shape of a volatile molecule may contribute to our perception of the quality of the odor.

PROPRIOCEPTION

The proprioceptive senses are especially designed to inform us of the movements and position of our body. These senses are divided into two groups, the *kinesthetic* and the *labyrinthine*.

Kinesthesis. Kinesthesis, the movement sense, tells us of the relative positions and movements of our limbs by monitoring the amount of stretch on our muscles and tendons and the degree to which our joints are bent.

Physical Stimuli. Kinesthetic sensations can be aroused by active or passive movements of joints, and by stretch and tension in muscles and tendons. Kinesthetic receptors also respond to changes in the tube-like internal organs of the body, for example the stomach and intestines.

Defects in Muscular Sensing. There are many aspects of bodily behavior to which man pays little attention unless they cause him trouble. One is unlikely to notice the importance of his kinesthetic senses unless they are impaired, for instance by disease. Then he must use vision to monitor the positions of his body members, a task which is not easy to sustain skillfully for long periods.

Upon damage to certain parts of the spinal cord, certain problems in proprioception will result. Without using his eyes, the individual will be unable to recognize the position of one of his limbs. He will be unable to recognize an object in his hand by touching it with his eyes closed. When standing with his feet together and eyes closed, there will be a significant amount of body sway.

Labyrinthine Senses. The labyrinthine senses appear to function principally to inform us of changes in speed of movement of our body through space in both linear and angular dimensions.

Physical Stimuli. The semicircular canals located in the inner ear are stimulated principally by change in speed of rotation of the head; the receptors in the vestibular sacs are stimulated primarily by changes in speed of linear movement, and presumably also by gravity. Extremely loud noises are also known to stimulate the labyrinthine receptors.

Receptors in the Labyrinthine Senses.

THE SEMICIRCULAR CANALS. (See Figure 16.) The three fluid-filled canals are approximately at right angles to each other and therefore can respond to rotation in any direction. When rotation starts or stops, or changes speed, the movement of the fluid lags behind that of the bony canal enclosing it. (You can see the same sort of thing happen when you rotate a glass of water, when at first the movement of the water lags behind that of the glass.) The resulting pressure bends the *cupula*, which is a jelly-like mass projecting from one side of the ampulla to the opposite side. Within the cupula are *hair cells*, the endings of the *vestibular nerve*, which are thereby stimulated when the cupula bends.

The Vestibular Sacs (Utricle and Saccule). (See Figure 16.) Within each sac is a structure called the *macula*, containing hair cells embedded in a jelly-like mass, on top of which is a membrane with embedded mineral crystals called *otoliths*. It is thought that a change in linear speed results in the otoliths bending the hair cells, thereby initiating nerve impulses in the attached nerve fibers. The force of gravity acts similarly.

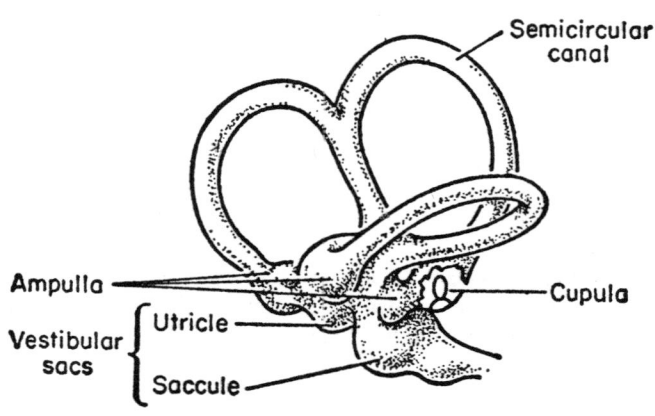

Fig. 16. Semicircular Canals and Vestibular Sacs

Stimulus and Sensation in the Labyrinthine Senses.   The stimuli for the labyrinthine senses have been described above; no sensation results from their stimulation. Instead, we are merely aware of changes in the speed of movement of the body, and its relation to the downward pull of gravity. In cases of malfunction of the labyrinthine receptors due to disease, a sensation of whirling called *vertigo* may result. In some disorders this sensation is accompanied by nausea. Long-lasting and unusual labyrinthine stimulation may cause motion sickness.

Chapter 8

Imagery and Cognition

Aspects of Thinking. The silent dialogue we hold with ourselves called *thought* is a complex, distinctly human activity. For the most part, mental processes are inaccessible to direct observation. The psychologist must therefore infer the content and nature of thought from what the thinker tells him. Just as our words cannot do justice to the vividness of our perceptions, so descriptions of thoughts, images, and concepts cannot do justice to the intricacy of our mental processes. Nor are we even aware of many characteristics of our reasoning. There are few obvious behavioral indications that we are thinking. Of course we may furrow our brow, scratch our head, or put our chin in our hand and thereby assume a contemplative appearance, but no one can observe what it is that encourages us to adopt this posture. We might be imagining ourselves skiing; we might be formulating a new scientific generalization; or we might be doing mental arithmetic—no one can tell. What people tell us about their imagery, thinking, or reasoning must be checked and supplemented by experiments. These experiments must be so planned that covert mental processes produce overt behavioral results on which to base inferences about mental activities. Psychologists concerned with various specific areas study these phenomena: the specialist in perception, the cognitive psychologist, the clinical therapist, and those researchers interested in growth and development. Each brings his own rationale and methods to the study of "higher mental processes."

IMAGERY

Sensory Images. Early in the history of psychology, there was a controversy over whether one could think without having sensations and images. The question had important implications for the group of psychologists known as the *structuralists*, because it amounted to asking whether all aspects of thought were open to detailed description by the thinker (the process of introspection). If some were not, then this basic method used by the structuralists could never yield complete results in the investigation of thought, one of man's most important abilities. At that time in the history of psychology, the structuralists were trying to account for every aspect of thought because the methods of the more rigorous physical sciences were thought to be useful to behavioral scientists. That is, just as the chemist attempts to determine all the elements in a compound and how they interact with one another, the structuralists sought to identify all the elements of a thought and their interrelationships. There was never any doubt that images often accompany thought, but several investigators independently concluded that imageless thought does sometimes occur. Thus the experimental laboratory added its evidence in support of the existence of mental processes of which the subject is not aware.

Afterimagery. After brief and intense visual, auditory, or cutaneous stimulation, a "copy" of the stimulus is recognizable for a fraction of a second after the termination of the stimulus. These persistent sensory images suggest that perception of such stimuli is not a passive process, but instead involves active "processing" of brief stimulus presentations. The intensity of these images is dependent upon the strength and duration of the stimulus.

Motor Images. Sensitive devices reveal that as one imagines himself performing some action, slight corresponding muscle movements occur, which are called *implicit* movements because they are too small to be seen. For instance, there are tiny movements in speech muscles when you imagine yourself speaking, tiny movements in arm muscles when you imagine yourself throwing a ball. Recent research has shown increases in neural activity in brain areas controlling voluntary movements just before these movements are actually carried out. It is as though the nervous system must first anticipate giving directions to muscles before it actually does so.

The Role of Imagery in Memory. When we are trying to memorize something, our task is often made easier if we visualize characteristics of the task in connection with some aspect of our environment with which we are very familiar. For example, if you are trying to memorize a few mathematical equations you might picture each one of them occupying a drawer of your desk, then you can mentally go through each drawer and "observe" the formula therein.

DREAMS

Research on dreams comes principally from two different sources, the laboratory and the psychoanalytic interview as first employed by Sigmund Freud. So far, the laboratory findings concern principally the nature of dreams, while the psychoanalytic research is about the meanings and motivations of dreams.

Laboratory Research on Dreams. With a high degree of accuracy, one can tell when a sleeper is dreaming by means of electrically recording his eye movements and the electrical activity of the brain. Both of these measures show characteristic changes when the subject is dreaming. This method does not disclose anything about the content of the dream, but makes it possible to waken the sleeper during or shortly after his dream to ask him about it. If too long a period is allowed to pass between the time a dream ends and the time the subject is awakened, he will not remember much of his dream. This method has yielded the following findings:

1) Dreams are rapidly forgotten. Fewer dreams are recalled if the sleeper is awakened later than eight or ten minutes after the dream ends. Apparently we remember best those dreams occurring just before we wake up. Several subjects in these experiments had asserted beforehand that they never dreamed, but were able to report dreams upon being waked up during the experiments. Apparently they ordinarily did not wake up soon enough after their dreams to remember them.

2) We dream several times each night. In one group of subjects, there was an average of half a dozen dreams each night.

3) Dreams occurring early in the sleep period, just after we go to bed, commonly concern current events in our lives. Those occurring toward the end of the sleep period, just before we get up, concern events and people we knew from earlier in our

lives. After one has been asleep for almost seven hours, dream content again returns to current events.

4) Dreams last about as long as they seem to. The dream actions described by subjects would require about the same amount of time to perform as the dream duration shown by the electrical recordings. It has been found that the length of a dream is directly proportional to the length of the sleeper's description of it.

5) External stimuli can cause some dreams. In some experiments, external stimuli were applied to the sleepers to find if the stimuli affected dreams. For instance, the sleeper's face might be sprinkled with cold water, or a gong rung in his ear. Such stimuli affected the dream content in about one-quarter of the attempts. Thus, sprinkling water on the dreamer might cause him to dream of being in a swimming pool, perhaps, or of walking through a summer shower; and the sound of the gong might result in his dream including a gong ringing.

6) Do we dream in color? The majority of the dreams have some color in them, although it may not be vivid.

7) Sleepwalkers and sleeptalkers have also been investigated in laboratory experiments. Both of these activities were found to occur at times when brain recordings and eye-movement records indicated that no dreaming was occurring.

8) Is there a need to dream? Suppose a number of people are waked up several times each night. Does it make any difference whether these interruptions occur between dreams or during dreams? It was found that repeated interruptions during dreams made subjects more tired and irritable the next day. When these people went back to sleep again, the frequency of their dreams increased, as if they had to make up for lost dream time. Sleep interruptions between dreams did not have these effects.

9) Drinking alcoholic beverages prior to going to sleep will cause a decrease in dreaming in the first few hours of sleep.

Psychoanalytic Interpretation of Dreams. Psychoanalysts distinguish between the "manifest content" of dreams and their "latent content." *Manifest content* refers to the content of the dream as described by the dreamer. *Latent content* refers to the inferred "real" meaning of the dream, in terms of the dreamer's own motives, of which he may be unaware. There is some disagreement about the validity of psychoanalytic inferences about latent content.

The psychoanalytic principle of dream interpretation is that most dreams express a wish by the dreamer, often in a disguised, symbolic form. Freud suggested that dreaming of that which we desire serves to preserve sleep and prevent waking.

For example, a little girl asks for a dish of strawberries, and is refused. That night, her wish is expressed in a dream, in this case undisguised, in which she is eating strawberries. In another example, a woman dreamed of the death of a close relative. This was interpreted as a disguised wish. Her "real" wish was not for the death of her relative, but for an excuse, such as the funeral would provide, to return to the town where this relative lived, because a young man lived there in whom she was much more interested than she knew.

Though psychoanalysts report that they find some dream symbols to have the same latent meaning for many people, their dream interpretations are principally based on the dreamer's associations to the content of his own dream and on the inferences he makes from these associations. Dream analysis is a commonly used psychotherapeutic technique; it can be an involved, arduous process, and may take a long time to explain a single dream.

CONCEPT FORMATION

Concept Defined. A *concept* is a classification based on one or more common characteristics. A symbol that represents a group of objects or events that are related to each other is a concept also. Examples: The concept of chair refers to a great variety of structures that have in common the fact that they were built to support the seated human body. The concept of red involves the characteristic that certain other objects have in common with a stoplight. The concept of gravity is inferred from the common behavior of objects which are free to fall. Concepts can be very broad, general, and inclusive, or very narrow and exclusive. Recognizing and using concepts is an important feature of thought and language; by doing so we note the commonalities and differences in groups of objects and words and their characteristics and meanings.

Studies of Concept Formation. Experimental studies of concept formation make use of the principles of discrimination and generalization referred to in Chapter 3. A series of stimuli is presented to the subject, his task being to recognize the concept exemplified. The subject must note what is similar in the presentation of stimuli of various kinds. In acquiring the concept of dog, a child notes those attributes of appearance common to all those dogs he has seen. If the child is confronted with a type of dog he has never seen and correctly recognizes that it is a dog, he has successfully generalized what he knew about other dogs to the new one. In the formation of a concept, repeated observation of members of a class of objects is necessary. Experiments with animals have taught us much about concept formation.

For instance, an animal may be taught to discriminate between a triangle and a circle. Once this discrimination is mastered, he is trained and tested on other triangles and circles—larger, smaller, inverted, of different color, and so on. If this training results in generalization such that the animal will make a correct discrimination between circular and triangular stimuli that he has never seen before, he is said to have mastered the concepts of triangularity and circularity. Animals can form this sort of concept, the complexity of the concepts that they can master varying from one species to another.

Frequently in experiments on human concept formation, the subject is presented with successive sets of stimuli in which any of several characteristics might represent the concept he is to form. For instance, a subject is presented with six inverted opaque cups in a straight line, underneath which are placed six marbles in varying positions. The experimenter has chosen a concept in which one cup remains empty, one cup contains two marbles, while the others contain one each. The position of the two-marble cup changes from trial to trial in an orderly way from the leftmost cup to the rightmost, one cup at a time. On trial one, cup one has two marbles; on trial two, cup two has two marbles, and so on. The subject has learned this concept when on six successive trials he can correctly predict which cup will have two marbles. On each trial the subject attempts to describe the correct concept and is told "right" or "wrong" by the experimenter. Problems more complex than this may be used, the stimulus series may include negative instances (the subject is shown sets that illustrate exceptions to the concept), and other variations may be made, depending upon the point to be investigated.

Under certain circumstances, the subject's behavior can be described as *trial-and-error*, if it is understood that this does not mean blind, random activity. The task demands the testing and revising of hypotheses, so it is not surprising that this happens.

Holistic and Partist Methods.   In the *holistic method* the subject at first assumes that all available characteristics of observable stimuli are relevant to the concept to be formed. At the outset of the experiment no information is discarded. When succeeding stimulus presentations demonstrate that some information is not needed in forming the concept, the subject stops attending to it. The subject's progress is slow and deliberate; however, the holistic method appears to be superior when the subjects are working under the pressure of time.

In the *partist method*, the subject picks one characteristic, and if a succeeding stimulus demonstrates its irrelevance, he drops the first characteristic and assumes that another characteristic contributes to a definition of the concept. When there was no pressure of time, subjects who adopted this method did about as well as those who adopted the holistic method; but under pressure, it was less efficient to place the reliance on memory which the partist method required.

It should be noted that concepts formed in the psychological laboratory differ from those we form in our daily lives, in that they are somewhat more simple and artificial.

Concept Formation and Cognitive Development.   Children form concepts that are qualitatively different from those formed by adults. By the time a child reaches the age of about nine, he can recognize that concepts such as number, mass, and weight are not dependent upon the physical form or arrangement of objects. By the time a child is twelve, he can put various objects in order along some dimension. Most concept formation in children involves only one dimension. It has been suggested that certain child-rearing environments, particularly cities, might require different concept formations than others, such as rural areas, might require.

Concept formation in adults usually involves more than one dimension, and the concepts are likely to be more schematic than those found in children. Adults use concepts to form other concepts.

THOUGHT

Thought is the symbolic manipulation of experience. Perception, memory, and concept formation are all important attributes of the cognitive process we call "thought." As was noted in Chapter 5, our unconscious thoughts can motivate our conscious thoughts. The degree of this unconscious influence is debated in psychology. Thought if in only loose contact with reality is *fantasy*. This is not to imply that fantasy is childish or counterproductive. Quite the contrary; fantasy is a sign of creativity and individuality. If thinking is relatively undirected it may be called *free association* or *reverie*. Thought may be directed at solving problems, as in *reasoning*. Thought can involve irrational, false beliefs as in the case of *delusions*. From time to time our thinking might operate in each of these ways. The majority of experiments on thought have involved giving subjects problems to solve and observing their behavior as they worked on them. Cognitive psychologists have designed experiments that allow them to make inferences concerning the nature of our thought processes when we are confronted with a variety of types of problems.

Human Reasoning.   Research on reasoning in humans has usually involved the presentation of problems that the subjects could not solve by the rote application of solutions from previous experience. Among the kinds of problems used have been mechanical puzzles, problems in inductive and deductive reasoning, and novel tasks of various sorts. Convergent and divergent thinking have also been studied. In *convergent thinking*, a problem is solved with the intention of deriving a single, specific correct answer. In *divergent thinking*, there are several "correct" answers to a problem. An example of convergent thinking would be the solution of a mathematical problem. An example of divergent thinking might concern weighing the possible alternatives one perceives in solving a personal problem. There are no "right" or "wrong" answers in divergent thinking, only more-or-less useful or acceptable solutions.

Problem Solving.   There are a number of factors and strategies in problem solving. The individual trying to solve a problem is often observed to go through the following three stages:

1) Preparation—exploring and analyzing the problem and

developing a hypothesis about how to proceed. Previous experiences with similar problems are recalled; old and new solutions to the problem are evaluated.

2) Attack—trying one or more methods of solution, varying these methods if necessary until a solution is attained. These hypotheses may be tested individually or simultaneously.

3) Evaluation—the solution is evaluated for its adequacy and revised if necessary.

Trial-and-Error. What we said above about trial-and-error also applies here. The subject may resort to guessing, meanwhile watching to see how a solution is attained if it is. Trial-and-error behavior in humans is characterized by hesitancy and irresolution in formulating and testing hypotheses.

Insight. In insightful thinking, solutions to problems become apparent suddenly and are correctly employed when the problem is confronted on other occasions. In some cases, the subject reports that the insight consisted of discovering the principle that would yield a solution when applied to the problem. Insights are frequently unexpected.

Past Experience. As was noted above, recall is important in concept formation; it is equally important in problem solving because a needed solution might be similar to one used before. Sometimes past experience can hinder the efficient solution of a problem, because it interferes with the adoption of the best method for the solution of the present problem. Whenever one hypothesis is exclusively used in the attempted solution of a problem, this strategy may discourage the formulation of other potentially useful hypotheses. Whenever we get "stuck" in working on a problem we are often encouraged to try a completely different strategy. Two examples of this kind of interference are called *set* and *functional fixedness.*

SET. Set is a predisposition to respond or behave in some particular way. No flexibility is involved. The detrimental effect it may sometimes have is illustrated by an experiment on the "water jar" problem. The typical water jar problem requires the subject to discover how one could bring back from a river a certain specified volume of water, with the aid of only two or three water jars of known capacities, none of which is the amount he is to bring back. For instance, how do you bring back 21 quarts if you have a 42-, a 9-, and a 6-quart jar? The answer is to pour water from the largest jar into the middle jar once and into the smallest jar twice, and then the required amount will be left in the largest jar ($42 - 9 = 33; 33 - 6 = 27; 27 - 6 = 21$). Subjects were given a series of problems with different numbers, but all involving this same routine. Thus they acquired a set to solve these problems in the same way. Then they were given test problems which could be solved in this way, but which also had a much easier solution. For instance, bring back 20 quarts if you have a 49-, a 23-, and a 3-quart jar. Because of the set acquired through previous experience with these problems, many subjects applied the habitual solution instead of switching to the quicker and easier one of pouring from the middle jar into the smallest jar once.

FUNCTIONAL FIXEDNESS. Functional fixedness indicates a lack of divergent thinking. Previous experience in using something for one purpose may prevent one from seeing that its use in a novel way can solve a problem. For instance, a subject may be very slow to solve a problem whose solution requires that he attach a pair of scissors to a length of string as a weight in order to form a pendulum. For some time he may think of nothing to do with the scissors except to cut the string.

Creative Thinking. Creative thinkers try to formulate something new. It can be an invention which makes our lives easier, a drug to cure an illness, a new technique in artistic expression, or a distinctive philosophical perspective. It is thought that creative ideas sometimes come into the thinker's conscious awareness after much unconscious deliberation; without knowing it, he can be working on the solving of a problem. There are no testing devices that we can use to try to find out whether or not someone is a creative thinker. Creativity is not related to standard criteria of intelligence or the scores one might achieve on a intelligence test.

There are stories told by famous creative thinkers about their own work which have led to the proposal of the following description of the stages of creative thought.

1) PREPARATION. One steeps himself in all the relevant information and ideas pertaining to the problem. One tries various methods, various solutions. If none of these is suitable, incubation follows.

2) INCUBATION. A period of little or no activity pertaining to the problem, perhaps for weeks, though some thought may be devoted to it now and then.

3) ILLUMINATION. A solution is obtained. It is often as-

serted that these solutions come suddenly, and sometimes that the problem is solved unconsciously.

4) VERIFICATION.   Often the solution must be tested and evaluated, sometimes revised, before it achieves final form.

Such observations are descriptive. Not much is known about the details of creative thought processes, nor about the causes of differences in ability to think creatively. We know that creative thinkers tend to have certain personality characteristics in common. They prefer the complicated to the simple and are very independent decision makers. They are somewhat assertive and have fewer inhibitions than most people. They are not necessarily well-adjusted, happy people.

Decision Making.   One facet of problem solving involves making decisions. What are the types of factors that enter into the making of a decision? Are we always aware of these factors?

We need to make decisions when we are confronted with choices. When two alternatives are relatively similar, our decision as to which to adopt is typically difficult and takes a long time. When two alternatives are apparently different, our decision becomes easier; we choose the more desirable of the two. By "desirable" we mean the one which most closely approximates our values and needs. In making decisions we reduce our uncertainty; decisions are more difficult when we lack sufficient knowledge to understand alternatives thoroughly, as well as the consequences of our choices. By delaying making a decision we afford ourselves an opportunity to collect more information. One particularly interesting aspect of decision making concerns the ways in which we perceive risks and what we do about them. It is thought that certain personality characteristics influence our willingness to take risks.

Decision Avoiding.   Some individuals consistently avoid making important decisions, although they may have no difficulty with unimportant ones. Decision avoidance strategies are commonly adopted. Some of us may make one important decision so that we won't have to make any others. For instance, we might carefully choose a spouse so that many important decisions in our lives can be referred to our marital partner and we won't have to handle them alone. We might embrace a religion that strictly dictates moral and ethical codes of behavior so that we won't have to decide our conduct for ourselves. We might affiliate ourselves totally with one political party and thus not have to evaluate each candidate on his merits at election time. From time to time we all employ decision avoidance strategies.

Information Processing. In all of our problem solving behavior we evaluate information for its truthfulness and utility in reference to a specific problem; sometimes we do this with a great deal of information. Some of this information comes from our memory; some comes from perceptual processes. An issue receiving much attention nowadays in psychology concerns the cognitive operations or steps employed in acquiring and using information to solve problems. It is thought that humans process information in a serial fashion, attending to "chunks" of information in a sequential order, using only a few images, concepts, or symbols at a time. Experiments have shown that our perceptual systems can process no more than about seven items at once. Our information processing abilities are therefore limited by our perceptual abilities, the capacity of our short-term memory, and the ease with which we are able to transfer information into long-term memory.

LANGUAGE

What are the processes by which we come to manipulate images and concepts and then communicate them in symbolic form? To what extent is this ability uniquely human?

The Development of Language. There exists a regular sequence of sound production in the acquisition of a language. Early in infancy babies babble; they produce a wide variety of seemingly random sounds. Some of these sounds will be used later to form words and others will not. The infant is able to give certain intonations to these sounds; there are declarative, interrogative, and exclamatory babbling sounds. Children first use meaningful words at around one year of age and almost all of these are nouns. This vocabulary of nouns grows very rapidly. Eventually the child begins to produce simple sentences by combining a noun with another word, commonly a verb: "doggie run," "car go." Between the ages of two and three the child produces three-word sentences. Cognitive growth is reflected in language complexity.

There are several other regularities in the characteristics of children's language. They almost always speak much faster than adults, and little girls develop slightly faster linguistically than little boys. When children mimic adult utterances, they reduce the length of the utterance but preserve its word order. For example, if an adult says "Where is the kitty's toy?" the child might repeat "Where kitty toy?" One question that has puzzled language theorists is whether children produce various aspects of language before they can comprehend them or whether production parallels comprehension. It appears that children from families of higher socioeconomic status develop linguistically slightly faster than those from families of lower socioeconomic status; the reasons for this are not fully explained.

Theories of Language Development. One popular view of language acquisition emphasizes the role of learning and the selective reinforcement of certain of the child's utterances and the nonreinforcement of others. Imitation of the language of others is important to this viewpoint. However, when we note how frequently adults use the various parts of speech (noun, pronoun, verb, adjective, and adverb), we note that children use them in very different proportions in their language. This would tend to de-emphasize the role of imitation in the development of language.

Another view of language acquisition holds that much of the child's capacity to develop language is innate, and the child develops his own ways to use and combine words. This position does not attribute great importance to the role of the environment. It has been pointed out, for example, that there are characteristics of language acquisition common to many different cultures with very different child-rearing environments. The role of maturation in this theory is very important.

Language and Animals. Subhuman primates do not have a vocal apparatus capable of producing speech as we understand it. But do they use the *rules* of spoken language to communicate in other ways? Several experiments have suggested that this might be the case.

A female chimpanzee named Washoe has been taught sign language by experimenters who never used spoken language in her presence. Training began when she was one year old and ended when she was five. At the end of the experiment she could understand several hundred hand signs, could use them herself spontaneously in combination, and could even occasionally "invent" a sign of her own. She could express parts of speech as well as concepts. Washoe's language development took place in a sequence very similar to that seen in human infants but required more time.

Chapter 9

Abilities, Aptitudes, and Skills

We all differ in our capability and our potential for completing certain tasks successfully. Some of these tasks directly concern our occupations and our suitability for them; some concern our avocational interests. One of psychology's major contributions to the behavioral sciences is the construction of tests that predict our performance on these tasks. Tests have been devised to measure what we can do, what we might do, and what we are truly interested in doing. Our productivity is enhanced if our individual differences are accounted for and impartially considered by those who seek to employ us. In this chapter the emphasis is on the ways in which individuals differ from one another and the procedures involved in documenting, measuring, and applying those differences.

TESTING OF ABILITIES

Since abilities are potentials for behavior, and are not directly observable, they are assessed indirectly. The individual performs a standardized task, under standardized instruction, and his performance is scored by a standardized system. His score is then compared with the scores of many others performing under the same conditions. Eventually a performance norm is established as well as percentile scores for substandard and superior performance. These are the basic principles of all psychological testing of abilities.

Validity and Reliability.   If test results are to be useful, they must be trustworthy. The *validity* of a test is the extent to which it measures what it purports to measure. The *reliability* of a test is the extent to which its scores are consistent; in other words, the extent to which it gives the same results when measuring the same quantities repeatedly.

A reliable test may not be valid. For instance, a reliable test that purported to test reasoning ability would be valid if it really did so, but would not be valid if scores actually depended solely on an ability to memorize. (In the latter case, the test could be used as a valid test of memorization, when research had shown what the test actually assessed.) An unreliable test cannot be valid, because scores on it are too inconsistent to be measures of whatever the test is supposed to measure. When a test is used for predicting performance on a criterion, the criterion measure—for instance, supervisor's ratings—must also be reliable. No matter how valid and reliable a test, it cannot accurately predict an unreliable, inconsistent criterion.

Once the validity and reliability of a test have been determined, some score is usually chosen as a cutoff point to limit the eligibility of the subjects for various training programs. In this way, performance on valid, reliable tests can be used to predict behavior on several kinds of tasks.

INTELLIGENCE AND INTELLIGENCE TESTING

Intelligence Defined.   Intelligence is commonly defined in any of several ways: 1) the ability to learn, reason, and understand; 2) adaptiveness to new situations; 3) a complex of abilities including verbal comprehension, reading, spatial visualization, etc.; 4) knowledge of a specific area of human inquiry; 5) that which intelligence tests measure. (This last is a conservative definition used by some who want to understand intelligence completely before defining it. It is analogous to defining "electricity" as "that which comes out of a battery." The definition doesn't tell you what it is, but tells you how to obtain a specimen of whatever was defined in this way.)

Intelligence Testing.

Test Construction.   In constructing intelligence tests, a very large number of potential test items must first be accumulated. They are evaluated for their appropriateness, and some are discarded. A preliminary version of the test is then drafted and administered to a large sample of people representative of the population that will eventually use the finished product. This sample should account for age, sex, race, and urban as well as rural subjects. Once the preliminary test has been given, standardized procedures for its evaluation must be adopted. The age level at which most individuals can correctly answer an item is also determined. Before the test is ready for general distribution, average test performance should be made to correspond to average scores on other measures of intelligence.

Types of Intelligence Tests. The well-known Stanford-Binet and Wechsler tests are *individual* intelligence tests, designed to be administered by an examiner in a highly standardized fashion to one person at a time. These two are the most widely used of the individual intelligence tests. *Group* tests are designed to be administered by one examiner to a large number of people at the same time, and are often of the multiple-choice variety, requiring the person tested to answer questions by indicating which of several alternative answers is correct.

The group tests provide an advantage in saving of time and in economy of testing large numbers of people. The individual tests provide a better check on the health and motivation of the person taking the test, on his understanding and carrying out of the instructions, and one other factors which might impair his performance.

The first successful intelligence test was devised by Binet and Simon in 1905 as a means of identifying those children in Paris who could not profit from conventional schooling. These tests have been translated and modified for application in other countries, being brought to the attention of psychologists in the United States by H. H. Goddard in 1908. There have been numerous revisions since then.

The Binet test and its early versions were originally designed for use with children, and only later were revisions made which extended the range to include adults. In contrast, the Wechsler-Bellevue test, issued in 1939, was designed for the testing of adolescents and adults, and only later was the Wechsler Intelligence Scale for Children published. The Wechsler tests include more nonverbal performance tasks than the Stanford-Binet. These tests involve the arrangement or manipulation of objects such as pictures and blocks. Wechsler test scores are very similar to Stanford-Binet scores for the same individual.

The impetus for the development of group tests of intelligence came from the need to classify large numbers of recruits during the First World War, and in the American army resulted in the development of the Army Alpha and Beta tests. The Army Alpha dealt with general intelligence testing, and the Army Beta was designed for people who cannot read or write English. Since then a number of group tests have been developed, often for specialized groups such as students entering college.

Rationale of Tests. All intelligence tests assume: 1) that those who take them have had equivalent learning opportunities; 2) that the more intelligent individuals will learn more from these opportunities than the slower individuals; 3) that the performance of those taking the tests is not impaired through poor motivation, misunderstanding of the task, and so on. If these assumptions are met, it is then to be expected that the more intelligent individual will be able to display more knowledge and problem-solving ability on the test than the less intelligent individual.

Schools have continued to be among the major users of intelligence tests. These tests indicate the potential of certain individuals to benefit from special learning opportunities; they suggest which individuals fall at the extremes on a continuum of intelligence ranging from the bright to the dull. Test results are used as screening devices to provide a rationale for admitting certain individuals into special training programs of one type or another.

Other Scales. We can learn more from scores on intelligence tests than a single index of the subjects' intelligence. Items concerning specific abilities can be grouped together and scored separately. In this way the subject's performance on such attributes as arithmetic skill, vocabulary, and comprehension can be assessed.

The I.Q. Knowing that a child's mental age was 8½ years would not ordinarily be useful unless one knew the child's chronological age. Then one could tell whether his mental age had kept pace with his chronological age, or was ahead of it or behind it. A score which has this information built in can be obtained by calculating mental age as a percentage of chronological age. The result is the so-called *intelligence quotient*, abbreviated as I.Q.:

$$\text{I.Q.} = \frac{\text{mental age}}{\text{chronological age}} \times 100$$

Thus, for instance, a 10-year-old who attains the average 12-year-old performance would have an I.Q. score of 120.

Growth in the abilities assessed by intelligence tests slows down, as physical growth does, when one approaches adulthood. This means that the I.Q. formula must be modified for adults, since the numerator stops increasing as they grow older but the denominator does not. The practice is to assign arbitrary chronological ages to adults, based on a table which compensates for the leveling off in mental-age scores. Thus I.Q. scores can be found for adults as well as for children, but in general it is more useful to express test results as percentile scores.

Percentile Norms. Most tests yield results in terms of percentile norms. Percentile norms relate one's test score to performance by the group on whom the test was standardized, thus providing a basis for interpretation of the score. For instance, to be told that you scored 37 points on a test tells you nothing. However, it becomes meaningful if you are told that this places you at the 80th percentile, that is, your score is higher than the scores made by 80 percent of the standardization group on this test.

What Do Intelligence Test Scores Predict? Our competence in school and various occupational settings has something to do with intelligence as we defined it earlier. But can our performance on intelligence tests *predict* the level of competence? There seems to be a relationship between various I.Q. scores and the level of academic achievement attained. Those individuals completing graduate school typically have higher I.Q.'s than those finishing college, and those finishing college usually have higher I.Q.'s than those finishing high school. However, personality and motivational factors, many of which cannot be measured, play a very important role in academic achievement. It has also been pointed out that individuals who do well in school perform very well on routine academic tests and these are very similar to intelligence tests.

Although psychologists have developed aptitude tests to select individuals with some potential for doing well in certain occupations, general intellectual ability also has something to do with a worker's competence. Individuals in some more advanced types of occupations ordinarily have a much higher average

I.Q. than those in other occupations. However, many individuals representing a broad range of I.Q. scores do well in the same job. The role of self-selection in occupational choice cannot be discounted, and personality and motivational factors are important.

Accuracy of Intelligence Tests.   Anything that affects performance on the test correspondingly affects the inference about intelligence which one bases on the performance. Inaccurate results may therefore be caused by illness, poor motivation, excessive stress, etc. As was pointed out in Chapter 4, for example, the level of difficulty of a task and the amount of arousal experienced by the subject work together to affect performance.

Since it is assumed that those taking the test have had backgrounds equivalent to those on whom the test was standardized, inaccurate results will be obtained for individuals with backgrounds differing markedly from those for whom the test is designed. So far, there is no intelligence test which has been demonstrated to be "culture-free" so that it could be used with groups differing from those on whom it was standardized. It is difficult if not impossible to account for differences in experience in different socioeconomic environments, and we should not lose sight of the fact that test scores will reflect differences in affluence, the availability of educational opportunities, and the type and amount of intellectual stimulation in the home.

Since the various intelligence tests do not give precisely equivalent emphasis to the various factors of intellectual ability, the results of one test are not perfectly comparable to those of another. Intelligence tests, like thermometers, show some variation from one to another.

Furthermore, there is some variability of intelligence test scores on the same test taken by the same individual at different times, even if the individual does not change meanwhile. For a well-designed test, most of this variation is within a range of roughly plus or minus 10 I.Q. points.

Testing Controversy.   The rationale and results of psychological tests have recently come under public attack. People are often mistrustful of unknowingly revealing information about themselves while taking these tests and feel that their privacy is invaded. Critics of psychological tests also believe that they unfairly discriminate against members of minority groups. People who take these tests do not like having the results withheld from them. The American Psychological Association has adopted strict ethical standards to ensure that psychological tests be not abused and that the tests be carefully designed, be given only when appropriate, and that no unfair inferences be drawn from the results.

Range and Limitations of Intelligence.

Nature of Intelligence.   Intelligence may involve both a general ability and a number of specific abilities. One individual can have little of some of these abilities, more of others, and still more of others, which means that they are separate factors in intelligence. However, there is some tendency for those who are better in some of these factors to be better in others as well, which means that to a certain extent a general intelligence factor is involved as well. Performance on individual factors is important to know about in counseling an individual concerning his educational aptitudes and vocational opportunities.

Exceptional Types of Intelligence.   Roughly 2 percent of children achieve I.Q.'s greater than 130. Roughly 3 percent of children score below an I.Q. of 70. What are these extremes of intelligence like?

The Mentally Gifted.   About 1 child out of 100 has an I.Q. above 140, and 1 out of 1000 has an I.Q. above 160. A disproportionate number of children of high I.Q. are from homes in the upper professional and business classes—more than five times as many as would be expected from their proportion in the population. This is thought to reflect advantages in both heredity and environment. The average parental intelligence tends to be higher in these groups, and the environment is likely to be a more stimulating one for the child. However, it is also true that mentally gifted children are found in homes in every socioeconomic class.

Though there are exceptions, these children tend to be very healthy, socially adaptable, good leaders, easy talkers, and great readers. As adults, a disproportionate number of them make outstanding contributions. The offspring of these adults have higher than average I.Q.'s.

The Mentally Subnormal.   Those who exhibit only the lowest degrees of intelligence are said to be mentally retarded or mentally defective. The mentally defective are sometimes further classified as follows. Morons develop into adults with mental ages of about 8 to 12 years; an imbecile's adult mental age is from 3 to 7 years; the mental age of the adult idiot is below 3 years. Mentally subnormal individuals are also classed as educable, trainable, and dependent. In most instances of mental retardation no specific physical cause is known. A general intelligence deficit is apparent; specific abilities do not selectively suffer. It is thought that social and cultural influences play a role in aggravating and perpetuating mental retardation. Hereditary factors are also believed to play a role.

Some types of severe mental retardation have known physiological causes. Sometimes they result from severe oxygen shortage—usually at birth—or from brain injury. Sometimes glandular disturbances such as a thyroid hormone insufficiency are responsible. Again, heredity is also thought to play a role. Inherited defects in body metabolism have been shown to have a relationship to certain kinds of mental retardation.

Dramatic improvements in the mentally subnormal are unlikely. Many of these individuals are quite congenial and industrious, with a strong sense of loyalty and responsibility. Most can be taught appropriate social behaviors as well as job skills. A good number of mentally subnormal are self-sufficient in adulthood.

For the most part, public school systems are able to attend to neither the special needs of the mentally subnormal nor those of the mentally gifted child. Our public schools usually design their curricula and offer instruction at a level of difficulty that is appropriate for individuals in the range of normal intelligence. Special programs of instruction are often necessary for the mentally gifted and the mentally subnormal.

Factors Influencing Intelligence.

Heredity and Environment. In intelligence testing, it is assumed that those tested have had equivalent opportunity to learn. How much measurable difference does it make if they have not?

Psychologists disagree concerning the relative contributions of heredity and environment to an individual's performance on an intelligence test. A rough estimate of the difference has been obtained by comparing the test scores of identical twins who, for one reason or another, were separated at an early age and reared under conditions providing quite different educational opportunities. Six such pairs of twins were tested. Because they were identical twins, the two members of each pair had the same heredity; yet in each pair one twin was raised under unfavorable conditions and the other under better conditions. On the average, those raised under markedly better conditions were

15 points higher in their I.Q. In contrast, the range of I.Q.'s in the whole population of this country, with all its differences in heredity, is about 200 points. Although six pairs of twins is not very many cases on which to base the comparison, it appears that differences in I.Q. result to some extent from environmental differences, but to a much greater extent from genetic differences. Individuals less closely related than identical twins can be expected to have I.Q.'s which differ to a greater degree, which indeed is the case.

There is one intriguing question of obvious importance in regard to different learning environments: What effect can be expected on intelligence test scores if children in impoverished environments are given special attention of one sort or another? There is diminishing optimism concerning these programs; it is unwise to expect any dramatic, measurable, or long-lasting benefits for every child who participates.

Malnutrition. Animal experimentation has shown that malnutrition prior to or during pregnancy has been implicated in substandard brain growth. It is not unreasonable to assume that malnutrition could have similar effects on the human fetus. Deficits in brain growth which occur prenatally cannot be compensated for after birth: brain growth cannot "catch up." Cellular and chemical differences are noted in these brains.

Race and I.Q. There have been a number of studies comparing the American white and black group average I.Q.'s. Much has been written about the possible reasons for the difference in average performance because it appears to be an appreciable one: 10 to 20 points. A number of difficulties arise in interpreting this information. Most intelligence test standardization has been done on white populations, so blacks are being compared to individuals who frequently come from very different environments. These different environments often provide the individual with different access to educational opportunities. Also, as was noted above, it is difficult, if not impossible, to find out how much of our performance on I.Q. tests is due to hereditary factors and how much is due to environmental factors. Much controversy has been generated by theorists who believe that the hereditary component is by far the more influential. The implication of this suggestion is that the reason whites perform better on intelligence tests than blacks do is because their heredity has made them more intelligent. Other theorists do not think that I.Q. differences among blacks and whites are due to genetic factors. It is unwise to draw any conclusions about racial intellectual differences by using I.Q. tests.

None of these findings are of use in dealing with individuals. The range of I.Q. scores of the two groups overlap to such an extent that an individual's racial membership provides no useful clue to his I.Q.

APTITUDES AND APTITUDE TESTING

Aptitude Defined.   Aptitude is the capacity to achieve skill in a particular endeavor as the result of training. For instance, when we say that someone shows a strong aptitude as a physician or as a welder, we mean that he will learn rapidly and achieve a high level of skill at these endeavors. Aptitudes are commonly thought of as our talents. As was pointed out in Chapter 2 in the case of the Bach family, the role of heredity is thought to be important in determining an individual's aptitude for certain skills.

Aptitude Testing.   The major purpose of aptitude tests is to determine who can profit from certain types of training. For this reason, aptitude test scores are useful to educational and vocational guidance counselors in assisting individuals in choosing a particular program of study or career. Aptitude tests, like intelligence tests, consist of standardized tasks performed under standardized conditions and scored in a standardized way. Often several aptitude tests are administered together; this is called a *test battery*. Aptitude tests are often printed tests on which the person being examined answers questions, but they may involve apparatus manipulation, or tests of factors such as color vision or physical endurance which may be required for success.

Constructing Aptitude Tests.   Since the items or tasks of an aptitude test must differentiate between those who will perform well and those who will perform poorly on the criterion, the validity of these items and tasks must be established. As it has been found that a single item or task rarely if ever makes this discrimination very well, a number of such items must be assembled into a test whose total score will discriminate better than a single item does. These are the reasons for the following procedure in developing an aptitude test.

1) Assemble a large number of items for the test. Since some of these items will not prove useful, more are assembled than will be required.

2) Test a large number of individuals with these items.

3) Assess each individual on the criterion. This means that all individuals, regardless of the score they achieved in step 2, must be given the training for which this aptitude test is being devised. Only in this way can those who succeed and those who fail in this training be identified.

4) Retain those items which the individuals who succeeded tended to answer differently from those who failed. Weed out those items which do not tend to discriminate between the two groups.

5) Cross-validate. With the retained items, repeat steps 2 through 4 with a new group of people. Some items which survived the first round did so by chance, and will not regularly discriminate between successes and failures. The cross-validation will weed out most of these items. The final form of the test consists of those items which survived the cross-validation.

Usefulness of the Test. No aptitude test discriminates perfectly between those who will succeed and those who will fail. What a good test can provide is an estimate of the odds for success. For instance, one can make statements like, "Of those who made the same test score as this man, 80% succeeded, 20% did not."

Types of Aptitude Tests. While aptitude tests can measure both verbal and nonverbal abilities, they are usually classed as being either scholastic or vocational aptitude tests, though the classification is rather arbitrary. Although certain aptitude tests are constructed with the intention of measuring or predicting a single type of skill (e.g., numerical), each aptitude is in some way related to one or more other aptitudes. This is the reason, as noted previously, that several aptitude tests are usually administered together.

SCHOLASTIC APTITUDE TESTS. Scholastic aptitude tests are intended to predict successful schooling. The conventional intelligence tests are an example. There are also aptitude tests for medical school, law school, graduate school, and others. These are *multifactor* aptitude tests, attempting to measure and predict several interrelated skills as opposed to tests concerned with single, specific skills.

VOCATIONAL APTITUDE TESTS. Vocational aptitude tests are designed to predict success in vocations not requiring extended professional training. For instance, such tests may be designed to predict success in becoming a radio code operator, a stenographer, etc. Vocational aptitude tests often consist of a battery of tests of various abilities such as verbal comprehension, mathematical ability, perceptual ability, finger dexterity, eye-hand coordination, and so on. Testing the individual thus yields a set of ability scores, called a *profile*, describing his relative standing in each of the abilities tested. Naturally not every ability is required in every vocation. In considering an individual's aptitude for a particular vocation, attention is paid only to those factors which differentiate successful people from failures in that vocation. Some vocational aptitude tests involve the evaluation of some behavior while the subject is doing it; other tests involve the product of the subject's work.

There is no evidence that vocational aptitude tests predict how far one will rise in his vocation. In part this may be because these tests do not assess factors of administrative and social judgment required at higher levels. In part it may also result from the fact that these tests cannot assess the specific situations in which the individual may find himself. It may be possible for an individual of given ability to advance more rapidly in one situation than in another. There may be better chances for advancement in a rapidly expanding company which is creating new executive positions than in a small, conservative company.

It is important to emphasize that any assistance derived from the use of vocational aptitude tests should not be interpreted as advice to be followed no matter what. People's abilities, interests, and levels of motivation change as they age, and this is quite normal, Also, different occupations and their attractiveness change through the years: new jobs can be created by pressing social problems and others become obsolete due to rapid technological growth.

VOCATIONAL INTEREST TESTS

What Are Interest Inventories and Why Are They Useful? Some of our most meaningful rewards can be derived from the feeling that we do our jobs well and that they are worthwhile. Yet many people are dissatisfied with their jobs. The vocational interest inventory is a tool that psychologists use to assist people in recognizing that their interests are very similar to those of individuals in certain occupations. There are several kinds of vocational interest tests. These are not aptitude or intelligence tests, and the items on them have no right or wrong answers. Vocational interest tests are revised and reissued frequently, as jobs and the people taking them also change often. For instance, recently women have been entering and succeeding in occupations in which only men used to work, such as medicine, law, and the physical sciences. Updated vocational interest tests are useful to guidance counselors in showing young women whether or not their interests are like those of other women who have succeeded in these occupations.

The Kuder Preference Test.   In the Kuder Preference Test the individual responds to a number of items in which he is asked to pick from among three alternatives the activities which he would like most and least. For example, one such item might offer him a choice between building a bird house, writing an article about birds, or drawing pictures of birds. These activities are specific instances representing general areas of interest such as mechanical, literary, and artistic. Other areas of interest represented include: computation, science, music, social service, persuasion, and clerical work. Scoring the test results in a profile of the individual's relative interests in these fields.

The Strong Vocational Interest Blank.   On the Strong Vocational Interest Blank the individual indicates his like, dislike, or indifference for a number of specific occupations, amusements, activities, and so on. There are almost 400 such items. The pattern of his answers is compared with the pattern of answers given by those who are already successful in one or another particular field; such as psychology, banking, farming, medicine, and so on. He is scored in terms of the similarity of his answers to those of successful people in each of these fields. There are separate comparison keys for men and women. Standardized test responses of successful individuals in over 100 occupations are available for comparison.

Possibility of Falsification.   Unlike ability tests, which require the individual to perform a task satisfactorily, interest tests ask him for a self report, which he can falsify to some extent if he wishes. For example, suppose an individual disliked the idea of being a salesman, but applied for such a job because he was desperate for work. If his prospective employer gave him a vocational interest test to see if his interests were suitable for a salesman's job, the man might decide to give the strongest possible impression that he enjoyed meeting and dealing with people. It is not hard to do this with at least some of the vocational interest test questions, and he could certainly have little difficulty in making the desired choice on such questions as:

Would you most enjoy:
                    writing an ad for a radio?
                    painting a radio?
                    selling a radio?

Consequently, interest tests are most useful in situations in which the individual is motivated to answer as truthfully as he can. Sometimes an item is stated in a slightly different form later on in the test to see if the individual answers it in the same way.

Changes in Interests.   The interests of children and adolescents often change markedly and repeatedly, which naturally diminishes the predictive usefulness of interest tests given at these ages. When interests have become more stable, it is not surprising to find that the chances of success in a vocation are better if one's interests are quite suitable to it than if they are not.

ACHIEVEMENT TESTS

Perhaps the most common kind of psychological test is the achievement test. Unlike aptitude tests, achievement tests are aimed at assessing an individual's present accomplishments, the level of expertise an individual has reached in a particular area of study. Achievement tests are widely used in education, industry, and government. The results of achievement tests can have a great impact on an individual's access to educational programs and occupational advancement, so it is very important that these tests reliably measure what they purport to measure. Achievement tests are also used as a means of assessing people who are to be employed without being given additional training. State bar examinations for lawyers and typing tests for stenographers are two examples.

Some achievement tests are not standardized, while some are. The standardized tests provide standardized instructions, tasks, and scoring, and yield scores expressed as percentile ranks. Course examinations in schools are common examples of unstandardized tests.

ADAPTING TASKS TO SKILLS

The emphasis in aptitude testing has been on finding the individuals with special talents suited to the requirements of a given task. However, the task is no longer regarded as imposing a fixed, unchangeable set of requirements; often there are advantages to be gained from redesigning the task so that effective performance is less demanding, as illustrated by time and motion study and by engineering psychology. Redesigning the work environment can enhance productivity and improve morale.

Time and Motion Study. As the name "time and motion study" implies, a careful study of job requirements is made in terms of activities required and the time spent on each. Time and motion study is used in those cases where a worker produces a tangible object which can be evaluated in terms of its quality and the time taken to produce it. For instance, in a particular manual task, one might find that 2 seconds were spent on each of these categories of activity: select, grasp, position, assemble, inspect, and wait—and that the left hand of the worker was doing only 20 percent of the work while the right hand did the rest. Further study might show that "select" could be eliminated from the series of operations and that "position" could be done in only one second if parts or tools were relocated, and if the task were redesigned in such a way that both hands could work simultaneously. Not all task improvements result from time and motion study, of course. Such simple things as changing a workbench to a better height and improving the illumination sometimes make a task much easier.

Engineering Psychology. With more and more machines of various sorts playing a role in our lives there has developed an increased interest in the requirements they place on the people who are operating them. Engineering psychology has developed to keep pace with these changing needs. One of its most important contributions has been in making it possible for tasks to be performed more easily and efficiently. The engineering psychologist studies all aspects of the work environment: choosing the best worker for a job, finding ways to keep him satisfied in that job, and finding ways to help him do his job easily and still productively.

Manner of Displaying Information. Many tasks require a man to make decisions on the basis of information displayed to him. It is therefore important that this information be displayed in a manner which he can readily and accurately perceive. An airplane pilot, for example, needs to know his altitude. Research showed that redesigning the conventional altimeter face made it much easier to avoid misreading the airplane's altitude.

Nature of the Required Response.   Many tasks require the individual to manipulate the controls of some device. Some types of controls and some types of manipulations tend to decrease the accuracy of response. If a small rotation of an auto's steering wheel turns the front wheels by a large amount, the driver can turn more rapidly but less accurately. The location of information displays and devices to be manipulated in the working environment have an important influence in determining the efficiency of a worker's labor.

Man versus Machine.   At certain tasks the human is inferior to equipment which can perform the same tasks. If a task requires maintained vigilance to detect something which happens only occasionally, man's efficiency at this task begins to drop very soon. It is difficult for a person to remember with perfect accuracy a large number of constantly changing bits of information, such as the exact location of all aircraft over the United States on a given day. Tasks of this nature are extremely monotonous and do not lend themselves to a high degree of job satisfaction. For this reason, computers are commonly used to do these tasks.

On the other hand, a person's capability exceeds that of machines in such areas as judgment and in reacting to unforeseen situations. It is the knowledge of the areas in which man is superior to machines and the areas in which machines are more suitable than man that enables us to make more and more efficient use of automation. Workers typically report a low degree of job satisfaction whenever their labors seem unrelated to or remote from the product of their work.

OTHER FACTORS AFFECTING PERFORMANCE

Motivational Factors.   It makes a difference whether an individual regards a task primarily as rewarding in itself, or as the means to be endured in order to reach a desired goal. In the first case, there is an *intrinsic* relation between task and goal, and the individual does the task as well as he can because he likes to do so. In the second case, the relation between task and goal is *extrinsic*, that is, there is an artificial relation between them. The individual who is paid to do something which bores him illustrates an extrinsic relationship. This is the sort of distinction which Mark Twain had in mind when he said that work is whatever you have to do, and play is whatever you want to do. About a third of the people working in the United States work in jobs that they do not enjoy.

Social Factors. In some situations, an individual's level of performance is largely regulated by social pressures. For instance, his fellow workers may have strong ideas about the quality and quantity of work it is proper for him to produce, and may exert pressure on him to conform to these ideas. In addition, the individual's performance can be affected by such factors as parental aspirations, his home life, and so on. In general, working with others will enhance the amount and energy of behavior, while perhaps making it less of an intellectual experience. The social rewards of interacting with others cannot be discounted in attempting to establish a pleasant, fulfilling working environment.

Chapter 10

Personality and Personality Disorders

Personality Defined. The concept of personality is a very broad one, and there are several definitions of it. Following is a definition which includes several of these variations.

Personality is the individual's characteristic (relatively enduring and predictable) organization (or patterning, or integration) of ways of behaving as he attempts to adapt to his changing environment and his changing relationships with other people. This organization of behavior takes into account an individual's aptitudes, attitudes, and acquired motives. It is essential to conceive of the personality as a fairly stable attribute of our outlook on life, but one which is still ever-changing in large and small ways.

Factors Contributing to Personality. There are important biologically and socially caused characteristics of our personalities. Our inherited predispositions, early life experiences, and physical maturation make important contributions. Our relationships with other people in a variety of types of social groups also have a great impact on the nature of our personality and its growth. Different antecedents of personality can be expected to result in different personality dynamics, and for this reason research concerning the area of personality causes, mechanisms, and measurement is an enormous task.

Approaches to the Study of Personality. There are two general approaches to personality research, one descriptive, one dynamic. In the *descriptive approaches* to the study of personality, the emphasis is on the individual's average behavior. The person is thought to have a number of *traits*, or enduring, predictable behavioral predispositions, which he is expected to display in a wide variety of situations. Some of these traits are assertiveness, shyness, imaginativeness, emotionality, and so on. There is no complete, definitive list of human traits, and all of us differ in the relative amount of each trait that is obvious in our behavior in most situations. However, our behavior in unpredictable situations often cannot be anticipated by knowing something about our personality traits. In addition to personality traits, the descriptive approach also deals with *personality types*. By giving a name to a group of related traits or predispositions, we simply are using a shorthand, summary term to describe a person's most obvious, visible characteristics. People are frequently called extraverted, introverted, submissive, and so on, to describe their most noticeable behaviors.

The *dynamic approaches* attempt to account for the individual's personality in terms of the interplay of his motives, experiences, and reactions. This is at once a more ambitious and a more difficult task. An individual is not always aware of these influences or the ways in which they determine his everyday behavior, and if he is aware of them and perceives them to be counterproductive, he may find it difficult to change their influence. In confronting and correcting personality disorders, an understanding of the dynamic approach is very helpful.

THEORIES OF PERSONALITY

Summarized below are some of the better-known approaches to personality. The descriptive approach is represented by type and trait theories, while the dynamic approach is represented by learning theory, psychoanalysis, and phenomenological theories.

None of these theories is more true or "correct" than any of the others. Each is only more or less *useful* than the others in describing and interpreting the personality. Each summarizes existing knowledge from its own perspective, suggests the nature of further work necessary for validation or refutation, and predicts the outcome of such further work. Each places different emphasis on the role of the unconscious, early childhood experiences, and our desire knowingly and willingly to pursue our own development and goals.

Type Theories. Strictly speaking, a type theory describes individual personalities as if there were only a few distinct categories of personality. An individual might be described as being either an introvert or an extravert, or as being either the brainy, brawny, or jolly type. Such personality descriptions are now felt to be inadequate because they leave out too many ways in which personalities differ, and also because personalities do not occur in such either-or fashion, occurring instead with varying degrees of a given characteristic. Type theories of personality are relatively useful and interesting because they suggest a few general schemes of behavior with a place for everyone; people approximate these general types more or less closely. Also, these types are fairly enduring, as the personality tends to remain fairly stable despite many different life experiences. The saying "people don't change" supports type theories also.

Because of the shortcomings of a pure type theory of personality, some type theories are modified to permit types to occur in varying mixtures and degrees within an individual, and to increase the number of types which may occur. In effect, they thereby become trait theories. A type may be conceived of as a special pattern of traits in an individual, seen in a number of people.

Trait Theories. Trait theories describe an individual's personality in terms of the relative degree to which he displays various traits or characteristics. For instance, an individual may be described in terms of his relative intelligence, perseverance, dominance, sociability, responsibility, excitability, and so on. The same individual will be evaluated in terms of the relative expression of these traits in differing social settings, as none of us is truly the same individual at all times. We all play different "roles" from time to time, so our traits cannot be considered without first finding out something of the surroundings in which behavior takes place. Some of our personailty traits may be strictly situational and others are thought to be more permanent, ingrained aspects of ourselves.

The principal research problem in trait theory has been to ascertain how many independent traits are needed for the description of personality. In order to do this, we must find out the degree to which different traits are independent of each other. It is not clear how many independent traits there are, but it is possible that there may be dozens.

Dynamic Theories. There are a number of personality theories which aim to account for personality in terms of processes and motives within the individual. This review briefly summarizes three theories of this type: learning theory, psychoanalytic theory, and phenomenological theories. As will become clear later in this chapter, these three theories of personality each employ their own therapeutic rationale for personality disorders. (It should be noted that "dynamic theories" is used by some authors in a more restricted sense as a synonym for "psychoanalytic theories.")

Social Learning Theory. In this approach, personality is to be understood in terms of principles of conditioning such as those described in Chapter 3. Classical and operant conditioning principles are employed in this kind of personality theory to explain the ways in which individuals acquire, maintain, or discard certain behaviors. Social learning theory also deals with what are commonly called *behavior modification techniques*. Principles of primary and secondary motivation as discussed in Chapter 5 are also incorporated into this type of personality theory. Characteristics of our personalities are acquired when we respond to information in our environment which reduces a drive (primary or secondary) and are rewarded for our response in some way. Such a reward makes it likely that we will continue using that response when confronted with that particular information. The principles of escape and avoidance conditioning are used to explain the ways in which we remove ourselves from situations in which something in the environment is unpleasant or punishing.

The parents who let a child have his way if he has a temper tantrum are reinforcing him for using this behavior to overcome obstacles, and because of stimulus generalization he would be expected to show this behavior in other situations. Thus, to understand the individual's personality, one must know the history of his conditioning. This is very difficult. As we pointed out in Chapter 3, we are always discriminating among stimuli, finding some of our behavior extinguished, and being frequently punished, and we operate under different reinforcement schedules.

Psychoanalytic Theory. Whereas social learning theory

stems from the principles of classical and operant conditioning as first investigated in the laboratory, the psychoanalytic theory of personality was developed from the observation of everyday human behavior, in large part from the treatment of emotionally disturbed people. There are various psychoanalytic theories, all basically similar, but differing in such ways as in the relative emphasis placed on cultural and social factors in personality development, or in the relative importance ascribed to various motives. The theory originated by Sigmund Freud, the founder of psychoanalysis, is fundamental to all psychoanalytic theories. (Psychoanalysis is also a term that refers to a form of psychological therapy, as we shall see later.)

The Freudian Conception of Personality Structure. Freud proposed three concepts representing major characteristics of personality structure. They are called the *id*, the *ego*, and the *superego*.

THE ID. The *id* represents instinctual desires and motives. According to Freud, we all have two basic instincts, sex and aggression. Id is blindly unreasoning. Id operates on the principle of "I want what I want when I want it." The young infant comes close to illustrating pure id in action.

THE EGO. The *ego* represents dealing with reality. The child learns that he must sometimes postpone gratification until later, that acting one some of his impulses can get him into trouble, that certain means are successful in accomplishing what he wants. It is inevitable that the ego will be in conflict with the id.

THE SUPEREGO. The *superego* represents the moral code and the ideas which the individual acquires. The superego is responsible for feelings of guilt and shame, and is often pictured as harsh and severe. While the ego would co-operate in stealing something the id wanted if there were an excellent chance of getting away with it, a strong superego would not allow this to happen, because it would make the individual feel too ashamed. Guilt is one of the most important motivators of moral behavior in society. The superego is thus in conflict with both the id and the ego. Sometimes the conflict makes us feel so uncomfortable that even the thought of transgression evokes feelings of anxiety and self-deprecation.

Since it is easy to personify the id, the ego, and the superego as if they were three little steersmen fighting within the person, it should be made clear that they are abstract concepts intended to summarize certain characteristics of personality.

The Unconscious.   Freud emphasized, but was not the first to suggest, that much motivation and much conflict is at an unconscious level, so that the individual is not aware of these factors. The id, and some of the ego and superego, are unconscious, and the conflicts among them may be unconscious as well. This prevents the individual from understanding himself completely. Freud thus stressed that man is not as rational a creature as he likes to think he is.

Personality Development.   Freud believed that the individual, in growing from babyhood to adulthood, successively attains three principal stages which he named to correspond to what he believed were the most important sources of gratification in each of these stages. Freud suggested the existence of a basic psychological energy which he termed the *libido.* As we develop, we invest libido in different parts of our bodies, the sources of gratification already noted. He called these parts of the body *erogenous zones.* In order, they are the oral, anal, and genital zones, each with its correspondingly named stage of personality development. The individual's psychological development can be arrested to some degree at any of these stages by environmental factors. For instance, if one were harshly weaned, there would be oral components in his personality as an adult, such as greediness and dependency. If harshly toilet trained, as an adult the individual would show characteristics of the anal personality, such as stinginess and compulsive neatness. For the adult to remain fixated at any of these earlier developmental stages would represent emotional immaturity. Reaching the genital stage is identified with achieving emotional maturity. (In some variations of psychoanalytic theory, there is less emphasis on parental handling of weaning, toilet training, etc., and more emphasis on parental attitudes such as love, rejection, and others which affect specific child-rearing practices and the way they are carried out.)

Freud believed that all children in all cultures develop through these stages, and he accumulated cultural, historical, and literary examples to support his theory.

Important Contributions of Other Leading Psychoanalysts.   Although recognizing the great debt they owed to Freudian theory, a number of major psychoanalysts developed concepts that were in some respects different from Freud's. Several of these analysts made decidedly important contributions to the field of psychoanalytic theory. Alfred Adler (1870–1937), once a student of Freud's, who founded the school of "Individual Psychology," originated the concept of the much talked-about *inferiority complex*, and investigated in detail the implications of that behavioral symptom. The nature of interpersonal relations and the impact of society on psychological development received much attention in Adler's thinking. Carl G. Jung (1875–1961), also a student of Freud's, focused his attention on the importance of *images* (the so-called father-image, mother-image, hero-image, and so forth), and considered the relation between personality and such spiritual areas as religion and mythology. It was Jung who developed the concepts of *introvert* and *extravert* types. Otto Rank (1884–1939) developed the theory of the *birth trauma* and its implications. Karen Horney (1885–1952) emphasized the important role that culture and society play in creating conflicts for the individual.

Phenomenological Theory. Phenomenological theory, also called *self theory*, emphasizes the way in which an individual views his own self, his ideal self, his world, and the people in it. This is an example of the humanistic perspective in personality theory. This humanistic emphasis assumes that we are free to make decisions concerning the direction of our growth. This perspective stresses that we are capable of becoming the best people that we can be, and conceives of the social learning and psychoanalytic theories as being overly contrived, with little room for the individual's appraisal of his own capabilities and deficiencies. While acknowledging that childhood experiences are important in personality development, the humanistic perspective holds that our perceptions of our immediate, current life situations are more significant. Self theory is concerned with the ways in which our views of ourselves correspond to our views of reality, and the ways in which our perceived selves compare with our ideal selves. The process of self-actualization is a part of humanistic theories of personality. This process involves the development of our full potential in life and a continual striving toward growth. The self-actualizing person realizes that he needs to be viewed with approval by society as well as by himself. He perceives reality accurately, is frequently a very creative person, does not feel compelled to "follow the crowd," and tends to experience life fully.

Comparison of Personality Theories. No one of the various theories of personality described has been shown to be clearly and overwhelmingly superior to the others. Each of the approaches mentioned, however, will undoubtedly contribute something of value to the development of a complete and widely accepted theory.

FRUSTRATION

Frustration Defined. Frustration is the interference with the achievement of a goal. Frustration may be caused by 1) environmental factors, such as when a traffic jam makes one miss his plane; 2) personal inadequacies, for example inability to master a course of training required for promotion; 3) motivational conflicts, such as when one wants to succeed but is afraid to try. We also become frustrated when we recognize some cue or sign that an obstruction can be anticipated, or some threat to our self-esteem. In order for frustration to occur, we must first see the achievement of our goal as being obtainable in view of our capabilities. Frustrations are unavoidable in our daily lives, and the ways in which we confront them and deal with them reflect much about our personalities.

Results of Frustration. Several factors determine our responses to frustration. For example, we must take into account the strength of our desire to attain the goal, the degree to which the interference seems insurmountable, the possibility of achieving substitute goals, the length of time that the interference has been present, and the degree to which small frustrations accumulate to produce significant frustrations.

A variety of reactions are seen in frustrated individuals, the particular reaction depending on the situation and on the individual:

1) Restlessness and tension.

2) Redoubled effort. Effort is intensified, or an attempt is made to find an alternative means of goal achievement. Frustration frequently energizes behavior.

3) Aggression. Aggression may be overt, in the form of actions or words intended to injure the source of frustration, or the aggression may be suppressed. Aggression is sometimes displaced, that is, if one cannot direct his aggression at the source of frustration, he directs it at something or someone else. For instance, the man who is reprimanded by his boss does not display his feelings at work, but instead might act unusually curt or touchy with his wife.

4) Depression.

5) Apathy. It is not known why some individuals manifest this reaction to frustration, one so very different from aggression, for example. However, a common reaction to longstanding frustration is indifference, accompanied by a lack of emotional expression. Experiments with animals have suggested that helplessness may be a learned behavior. This is an interesting notion in view of the nature of the behavior seen in individuals hospitalized with personality disorders.

6) Regression. Sometimes frustration results in a reversion to earlier habits of behaving or to behavior which is more primitive or childish.

7) Fantasy. When realistic attempts to achieve a goal fail, an individual frequently tries to acheve the goal in his imagination. Both children and adults fantasize in this way.

CONFLICT

The Nature of Conflict. Motivational conflict results from the simultaneous occurrence of desires which cannot all be achieved. The conflict is frequently the cause of frustration. No goal that we seek to achieve is completely positive, without any negative aspects; all goals have both characteristics. For this reason, we often hesitate in deciding which goal to try for and how to go about it. Different personality theories have quite different things to say about this situation. The social learning theorist maintains that our behavior in the face of conflict is easily predictable in view of the nature and amount of reinforcement gained by achieving our goal, or the nature of the punishment we have experienced in the past by not achieving our goal. Our "reinforcement history" is important to the social learning theorist. Psychoanalytic theorists often suggest that much of our conflict derives from a discrepancy between the superego and the ego acting with the id. This implies that many of our conflicts come from some motives of which we are unaware. Humanistic theorists might argue that the emotional aspects of previous reinforcements are important, and that we have more awareness of our motives than psychoanalytic theorists believe. The humanistic theorist believes that many of our conflicts stem from our inability or unwillingness to recognize both desirable and undesirable aspects of goals and to make a responsible decision about what to do in view of the way we perceive the situation.

It is convenient to analyze conflict in terms of two kinds of behavior toward goals: approach and avoidance. In connection with positive, desired goals there is an "approach gradient," in connection with negative, repellant goals there is an "avoidance gradient."

Approach and Avoidance Gradients. Approach and avoidance gradients are graphically illustrated in Figure 17. As one gets closer in time or in space to a positive goal, the strength of the tendency to approach it increases. As one gets closer in time or in space to a negative goal, the strength of the avoidance tendency increases. The avoidance gradient is generally steeper than the approach gradient, meaning that avoidance tendencies increase more rapidly than approach tendencies do as one nears the corresponding goals. The dashed lines indicate the raising of these gradients by increases in motivation. These gradients are used in the analysis of various kinds of motivational conflict.

Approach-Approach Conflicts. In an approach-approach conflict (one that is between two desired but mutually exclusive goals), the individual is at the intersection of the two approach gradients. As soon as something happens either to change his location slightly or to shift one of the gradients slightly, he will move toward one of the goals. Thus, in this type of conflict there may be an initial period of vacillation but the conflict will be resolved rather readily. A hungry donkey between two bales of hay will not need much time to resolve his approach-approach conflict.

Approach-Avoidance Conflicts. This type of conflict occurs when the same goal has both positive and negative characteristics and the resulting approach and avoidance gradients intersect. The little boy who wants to wade in the ocean but is afraid of the waves is in this sort of conflict. At a distance from the goal the approach tendencies are stronger than those for avoidance, but as he nears the goal, the avoidance tendency becomes stronger than that for approach, and he retreats. This state of conflict persists until something happens to change the gradients or to remove the individual from the conflict.

Avoidance-Avoidance Conflicts. In this case both goals are negative, and in the absence of anything to prevent his doing so, the individual will "leave the field," that is, remove himself

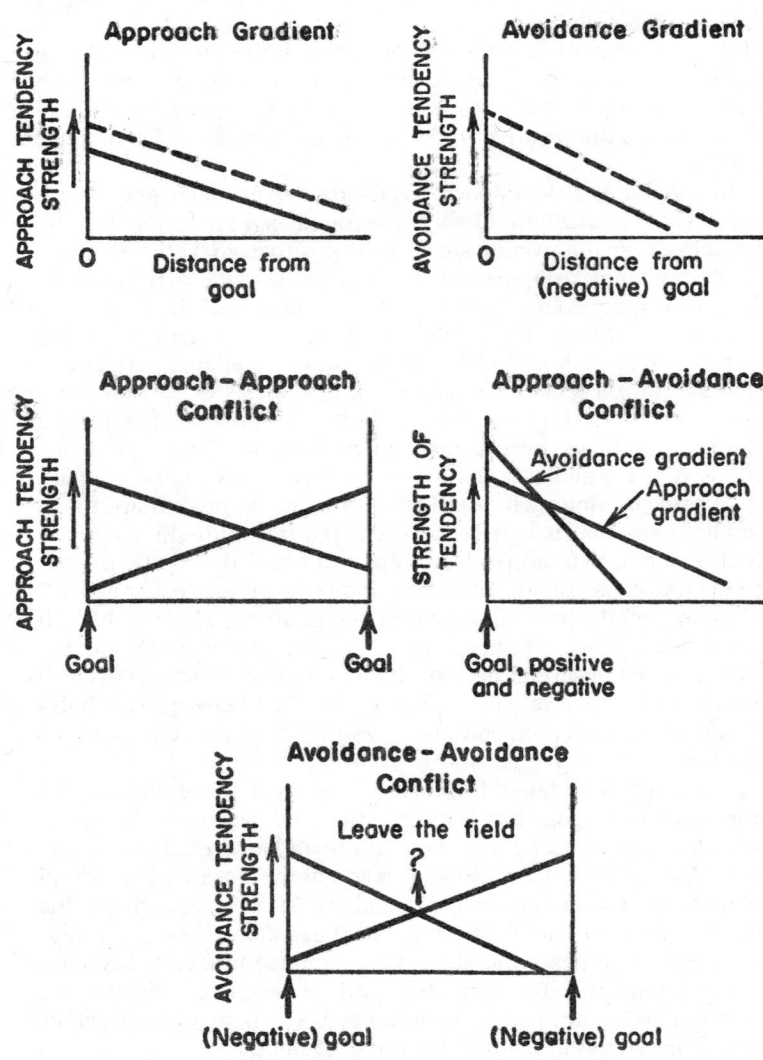

Fig. 17. Approach and Avoidance Gradients

from the vicinity of both negative goals. The situation becomes one of conflict if he cannot use this solution. Then, in order to avoid either negative goal, he would have to approach the other negative goal. Avoidance-avoidance conflict is illustrated by the child who will be spanked if he does not eat a food he hates. If he is not allowed to leave the field, his only choice is either to take the spanking, or to force down something he dislikes. Since approaching either negative goal increases the strength of the tendency to avoid it, he is likely to do neither, unless the severity of threat of punishment is increased to the degree at which its avoidance gradient is higher throughout than the other avoidance gradient.

In understanding conflict caused by frustration and the ways in which this conflict motivates our behavior, it is important to keep in mind the relationships among a number of factors. Different types of conflict present the individual with different numbers of alternatives, and this results in resolutions of varying degrees of certainty. These factors in turn directly affect the amount of time the individual requires to reach his decision. While the types of conflict noted above appear to be relatively straightforward, in actuality our daily lives include a number of approach-avoidance conflicts with several alternatives, and these may require a lot of time to reach a decision.

DEFENSE MECHANISMS

Defense Mechanisms Defined.   Motivational conflict can lead to *anxiety*, a feeling of apprehensiveness that is not attached to any specific, observable stimulus as fear is. When anxiety is strong it can be extremely unpleasant. Some of our anxiety occurs for good reasons; we can expect to feel anxiety when we realistically appraise various threats in our environment. But some anxiety is of an unconscious origin, in which event we don't know its cause. Because anxiety is so unpleasant, we try to do things to reduce or do away with it. Some of our techniques of doing this are consciously motivated, others are unconsciously motivated, and among the latter are the defense mechanisms. These are techniques by which individuals conceal from themselves knowledge of the existence or strength of motives whose recognition would be unpleasant. References to the kinds of behavior now called "defense mechanisms" occur in many early writings, but psychoanalytic theory was responsible for the systematic exposition of these mechanisms.

Defense mechanisms appear to be used to some extent by practically everyone at one time or another, and when used in moderation appear to be a normal mode of adjustment. It should be emphasized that true defense mechanisms are not consciously and deliberately employed; some degree of self-deception is involved.

Types of Defense Mechanisms. The principal types of defense mechanisms are: repression, rationalization, projection, reaction formation, displacement, compensation, sublimation, and identification.

Repression. Thoughts and feelings which would arouse anxiety if the individual were aware of them are not allowed into consciousness. Example: An individual who hates his father without knowing it. Repression is the process by which we keep things from consciousness without being aware of it. This is different from *suppression*, the process by which we consciously deny impulses.

Rationalization. One believes that his behavior results from some motive other than the true one. Rationalizations are commonly excuses. Example: An individual who believes that he declined to compete because the prize was not worth winning, not because he was afraid of failing.

Projection. One's own motives or characteristics are ascribed to others. Example: A selfish individual who believes that other people think only of themselves.

Reaction Formation. An undesirable motive is overcome by an excess of its opposite. Example: A mother, to avoid realizing her hatred of an unwanted child, overwhelms the child with solicitous care.

Displacement. The true goal of a motive is replaced by another goal. Example: A man who is afraid to beat his wife beats his horse.

Compensation. The individual tries to excel in some way in order to make up for a real or imagined defect. Example: A boy, smaller than average, becomes the best fighter in the area.

Sublimation. A proposed mechanism in which a substitute activity serves to gratify a sexual drive originating in the developmental stages prior to the mature (genital) stage. The drive is thus desexualized and deflected to another goal, but it is not blocked. Example: The activities of the scientist or of the reporter are interpreted as being sublimation of the child's desire for sexual knowledge. (The validity of this concept has been questioned.)

Identification. One acts as if in certain respects he were somebody else. Identification is thought to occur both as a defense mechanism and as a normal process in socialization.

Example of identification as a defense mechanism: The rather timid man who takes great pride in the victories of the boxing champion, as though he himself were an aggressive, fearless winner.

Example of identification as a normal process in socialization: The little girl who plays house, thereby showing that she identifies with her mother. Identification is a factor in socialization because it leads the child to initiate adult behavior.

Consequences of Using Defense Mechanisms. The function of defense mechanisms is to prevent or minimize discomfort resulting from psychological conflict, but the use of defense mechanisms does not resolve the conflict, and in the long run it may prevent our realistic perceptions of situations. If the conflict is a mild one, or can be resolved without special attention, use of defense mechanisms may serve a useful function in decreasing the discomfort. If the conflict is severe, however, so that defense mechanisms are strongly used, they serve only to provide an unrealistic concealment of the extent of the problem. In addition, their excessive use can result in behavior which is undesirable from the viewpoint both of the individual and of other people. For example, a man whose projection takes the form of constantly accusing others of secretly disliking him not only is unpleasant to associate with, but also is behaving in such a way that the imagined dislike on the part of others will become a reality. Excessive use of defense mechanisms inhibits creative problem-solving behavior, and the motive which first instigated the use of a defense mechanism is never really satisfied.

Defense mechanisms are not all bad. They provide the individual with a means for coping with his problems without having to deal with them immediately each time they emerge. Also, our level of maturity is not always commensurate with an ability to deal with some of the problems which we confront, and defense mechanisms provide us with a growth experience in which we view ourselves in new ways. They are not always a sign of weakness and immaturity.

PERSONALITY DISORDERS

The Two Principal Types of Personality Disorder. A *neurosis* is a moderate form of personality disorder; a *psychosis* is a severe form of personality disorder. The neurotic is in better touch with reality than the psychotic. These terms are nonjudgmental; neurotic and psychotic individuals are not necessarily bad or dangerous people. It is estimated that there are at least ten million neurotics and one million psychotics in the United States today, requiring different types of therapy at a tremendous cost in money and in loss of productivity.

Neurosis. (Psychoneurosis; Psychoneurotic Reaction). A neurosis is a moderate personality disorder, seldom disabling or dangerous, but certainly troublesome. Neurotic behavior is commonly characterized by a number of persistent indicators of maladjusted behavior of which an individual may be unaware or which he may be unable to discard. Neuroses are generally considered to result from conflicts of whose existence or strength the individual is not conscious. The symptoms differ in degree, rather than in kind, from characteristics of the normal individual. Therefore, the presence of the symptoms outlined below does not automatically indicate that a person is neurotic, and diagnosis should be left to the experts.

There are a number of ideas about the ways in which people acquire neuroses. Some of these include arrested psychological development and an inability to dissipate guilt, having to live under conditions of extreme stress in family, job, or social group, or the existence of learned behaviors which detract from effectiveness in interpersonal relations.

It is convenient to present the description of neurotic symptoms by categories. Actual neuroses are not always so neatly packaged, however, and mixtures of symptoms can occur.

Anxiety Reaction. Anxiety is the most common neurotic symptom. The person has all the signs and feelings of strong fear, without being aware of a cause. Sometimes he is not aware even of his anxiety, but has only the appropriate bodily symptoms, such as perspiration, a racing heart, etc.

Obsessions, Compulsions. An obsession is a thought which keeps intruding into one's mind, for example, the thought that one is in constant danger from deadly germs. A compulsion is an action which must be carried out repeatedly, such as washing one's hands more than a hundred times a day. An obsession and a compulsion may be related, as in the examples just given, or there may be a compulsion without a corresponding conscious obsession. The individual with these symptoms understands that his behavior is irrational. Obsessions and compulsions are often trivial and harmless and it is thought that they may be reaction formations that an individual uses to keep from seeing his own real motives. These motives may involve dangerous impulses.

Phobias. A phobia is an unusually strong fear of a specific thing of situation, such as a fear of enclosed spaces or a fear of water. In some cases the fear is of the same thing which originally caused the phobia, although the person is not aware of this relation. In other cases the fear has been displaced from its true cause to something else. The individual experiencing a phobia greatly exaggerates the danger of the feared object. Phobias are not difficult to adjust to; individuals know those things which elicit intense fear and they stay away from them.

Depressive Reaction. Neurotic depression involves an individual's exaggerated dejection and sadness in response to some transient stress. The depressive reaction typically lasts a long time. Difficulty in concentration and insomnia often accompany this neurotic symptom.

Disturbances of Memory and Consciousness. *Amnesia* (loss of identity), and *fugue* (flight), are two illustrations of memory and consciousness disturbance. In amnesia, one cannot remember who he is, and may also forget his family and friends. In fugue, the individual finds himself somewhere with no recollection of how he got there, or of the sometimes very complicated sequence of actions which he took to get there. Individuals with multiple personalities are examples of fugue states. Amnesia and fugue are fairly rare neurotic symptoms.

Bodily Symptoms. The following neuroses emphasize physical symptoms.

CONVERSION REACTION. (This is sometimes called conversion hysteria, but note that the term hysteria does not have the everyday meaning of an uncontrolled emotional outburst.) There is a bodily symptom for which there is no physical cause. For instance, one hand may be totally insensitive, but the area of insensitivity may be one which no physical lesion can produce (so-called *glove anesthesia*). It is thought that the motivation for the appearance of these ailments lies in our withdrawal from anxiety-arousing situations due to illness. The sympathy we derive from these symptoms is also considered an important reward.

HYPOCHONDRIA. An excessively intense concern with and fear about one's health, often in spite of medical assurance of good health. The individual consistently refuses to recognize that his illness may be caused psychologically; sympathy and attention are important to him.

NEURASTHENIA. Excessively great fatigue, which cannot be accounted for by medical or physical reasons. This symptom is commonly seen in highly dependent, immature individuals.

Comments on Neurosis. First, it will be noted that many of the symptoms just described as being psychologically caused, and also symptoms resembling them, could also result from physical illness. In any given case, careful study is required before an accurate diagnosis can be made.

Secondly, the genuine neurotic is not shamming. Although there may be no physical cause for his physical symptoms, although his fears may seem grossly unreasonable to us, he is not consciously attempting to deceive us.

Thirdly, little is to be attained by attempting to cure symptoms without resolving the conflicts which produce them. Trying to reason an individual out of his phobia or argue him out of his obsession does not get at the root of his difficulty.

The neurotic is caught in a situation called the *neurotic paradox.* The individual feels that he is incapable of confronting and solving common problems; he uses defense mechanisms to help him do so; he continues to feel inadequate because he does not solve his problems using a direct, rational approach. The neurotic sees what he is doing and cannot change. Also, the neurotic individual is commonly very egocentric; he is incapable of perceiving events or the feelings of others from any perspective but his own.

Psychosomatic Illness. In some cases, psychological tensions are contributing factors in such genuinely physical ailments as ulcers, asthma, headache, and others. This is not surprising, since it is known that emotion can affect bodily processes. On the other hand, it is certainly not true that these ailments are always psychologically caused. It is commonly thought that psychological stress can precipitate physical illness. We all react to stress differently, and if one of our body's organ systems is repeatedly the target of emotional tension we can expect that particular organ system to be the first to show signs of wear and tear. Whether or not people with specific types of personality are prone to manifest specific psychosomatic disorders is an issue still open to question.

Psychosis. Psychosis is a severe personality disorder which often, though not invariably, requires that the psychotic individual be placed under care for his own protection or for the protection of others.

In everyday language, "*insanity*" is often incorrectly used to mean psychosis. Insanity is a legal term, not a medical one. In most jurisdictions, a legal defense on the ground of insanity requires proof that "at the time of committing the act the party accused was laboring under such a defect of reason from disease of the mind as not to know the nature and quality of the act he was doing, or, if he did know it, that he did not know he was doing what was wrong." A psychotic person might legally be either sane or insane.

Some kinds of psychoses are frequently accompanied by delusions or hallucinations or both, others rarely are. *Delusions* are beliefs which to normal people are obviously false, such as that one is the queen of Rumania, or that the kitchen is full of congressmen poisoning one's food. *Hallucinations* are perceptual experiences which to normal people are obviously false, such as hearing voices inside one's head constantly rebuking one, or seeing everybody with animal heads instead of human ones.

It is again a convenience in presentation to categorize the description of psychotic characteristics.

Psychoses are conveniently divided into two types. *Organic psychosis* is a psychosis for which a physical cause is known; *functional psychosis* is a psychosis for which no physical cause is known, and which is therefore thought to be an extreme psychological reaction. While the neurotic individual is trying to cope with his own distorted perceptions of reality, the psychotic isn't trying anymore. When confronted with the notion that he might be ill, he denies it.

Organic Psychoses.

ARTERIOSCLEROTIC AND SENILE PSYCHOSES. Sometimes the processes of aging result in a defective blood supply to the brain. If severe enough, this may result in disturbance of memory, difficulty in sustaining effort, emotional irritability and instability. Sometimes there is sexual misbehavior.

ALCOHOLIC PSYCHOSIS. Severe prolonged alcoholism may result in brain damage and symptoms like those of arteriosclerotic psychosis. In addition, there may be bouts of acute fear.

GENERAL PARESIS. Now and then syphilis results in damage to brain tissue, often many years after the disease first presented its symptoms. Untreated general paresis is frequently fatal. In addition to having various physical symptoms, the individual may be irrational, depressed, or have a feeling of excessive well-being, or show much agitation. Contact with reality is lost and there are often delusions. There is no cure for the advanced stages of general paresis.

Functional Psychoses.

MANIC PSYCHOSIS. Manic psychosis is characterized by great elation, rapid flight of ideas, and quick physical action. The individual is very talkative and often designs extravagant schemes that are expensive and unrealistic. There are mild and extreme forms of mania, the latter being rarer and involving a greater potential for injury to the patient or others. The individual may be very irritable if thwarted in any way.

DEPRESSIVE PSYCHOSIS. In depressive psychosis, the individual speaks slowly and sadly, has great difficulty in thinking, and is slow to move. He has feelings of low self-esteem, and may even attempt suicide. People with this disorder become depressed for no apparent reason; the depression is likely to recur periodically.

Some individuals exhibit symptoms of both manic and depressive psychoses in a cyclical fashion, swinging from one extreme to the other unpredictably.

SCHIZOPHRENIA. Schizophrenia is the most common of all the psychoses. These are several subcategories of schizophrenia, which have in common that the individual shows dulled and grossly inappropriate emotional reactions. The individual is not in contact with reality, and often experiences delusions and hallucinations. The schizophrenic's behavior appears very strange, often including shouted obscenities, unusual gestures, or total immobility for long periods of time. It is thought that the schizophrenic cannot sort out important from unimportant stimuli, and that these get mixed up with each other. For this reason, speech seems illogical and disorganized. Most schizophrenics are young adults. This psychosis can be the result of an extreme reaction to some situational stress or can evolve slowly over a number of years.

The *simple schizophrenic* is apathetic, withdrawn, and emotionally dulled.

The *paranoid schizophrenic* has delusions of persecution or grandeur, and, frequently, vivid hallucinations, which often are auditory. The paranoid is extremely suspicious and hostile.

The *catatonic schizophrenic* is withdrawn, may give the false appearance of being in a stupor, and may hold a given position for hours. Catatonic schizophrenics experience extreme mood swings, and cannot care for themselves.

The *hebephrenic schizophrenic* shows some characteristics of other types, but a prominent characteristic is silliness. They often talk to themselves and display very unusual gestures and speech mannerisms, inventing their own bizzare, meaningless expressions.

Comment on Psychosis.   It has not yet been agreed whether functional psychosis differs only in degree, or also in kind, from neurosis. In order to better understand this issue we will discuss three types of theory about the causes of functional psychosis. These are the biochemical, the genetic, and the psychological.

The *biochemical theory* is that functional psychoses will turn out to be organic, resulting from some disorder in the biochemistry of the cental nervous system. There are no firm data that support this theory; no biochemical disorder has been found, but research in this direction is continuing. It is very difficult to be able to say that something in the blood of a schizophrenic not found in the blood of normal individuals is a cause of his aberrant behavior, rather than a result of his being so emotionally upset. Finding a biochemical correlate of schizophrenia in the form of some single substance in the blood would be surprising in view of the diversity of behaviors we call schizophrenia.

The *genetic theory* holds that a predisposition toward functional psychosis can be inherited. In an often-cited study, there was compared the incidence of schizophrenia in fraternal twins to the incidence of schizophrenia in identical twins. It was found that if one *fraternal* twin had schizophrenia, in 14 percent of the cases the other twin had it also; if one *identical* twin had schizophrenia, the other twin also had it in 86 percent of the cases. For various reasons, these figures cannot be taken as being precise, but they do indicate an effect of inheritance on the incidence of schizophrenia. Schizophrenia itself is not inherited, but resistance of factors tending to cause schizophrenia can be affected by one's genetic makeup.

The *psychological theory* holds that something in early child-parent relationships may bring about schizophrenia. No single, specific type of family has been proven to predispose children toward schizophrenia. It is still difficult to say why some individuals fall victim to schizophrenia, while others in apparently similar circumstances do not.

PSYCHOLOGICAL THERAPIES

Methods of Treatment. There are a number of approaches to the treatment of psychoneurosis and psychosis, though the methods discussed below are not mutually exclusive. One method emphasizes physical treatment and telling the patient what to do; another stresses resolution of conflict, achievement of insight, and acceptance of self, and avoids telling the patient what to do; and a third approach emphasizes the recognition of factors in the patient's social environment which produce conflicts, and it attempts to alleviate these factors.

These therapies can be carried out either while the individual is hospitalized or is an outpatient, and may be undertaken by psychiatrists, clinical psychologists, or specially trained laymen, either working on a *one-to-one* basis with the patient or with one therapist interacting with a *group* of patients in an informal meeting. In the group, patients can help other patients by supporting them or by pointing out problems of which they are unaware. Very frequently a *team* of professionals will treat the same patient: a physician may deal with a patient's ulcers, a psychiatrist with the patient's perceptions of conflict-producing situations, and a social worker with helping the patient get another, less stressful job. This is called the *holistic approach*, because the total individual, and not just his psychological difficulty, is studied in the therapeutic setting.

People, like lower animals, each live in their own ecological niche. Our health and effectiveness are determined by many factors which interact with each other so that we can maintain some stability in our niches. *Community psychology*, a relatively new branch of psychology, concerns the ways in which an individual with problems can be helped before it becomes necessary to begin a formal therapeutic program. Community psychologists are interested in making more people aware of the fact that they are not the only individual with a certain problem, that some problems are extremely common, and there are ways to deal with them. *Crisis intervention* telephone programs have been very helpful in this respect.

Several themes are common to people's motivations in seeking psychological therapy. It is difficult to make a complete list of problems which prompt people to seek help, but some frequently noted difficulties include: sexual problems and gender identity, confusion, difficulty in establishing and maintaining love relationships, maladaptive dependency tendencies, difficulty in coping with aggressive feelings or an inability to express them when it is appropriate, difficulty in coping with stress which might come from one's job or family, or difficulty in adapting to the death of a loved one. These problems do not necessarily require long-term therapy, and may improve markedly after only a few counseling sessions. Much depends on the patient's motivation to get better and the degree to which his insights into his problems are accurate.

Physical Treatment. Antidepressant, tranquilizing, or other drugs may be given, together with advice. The widespread use of tranquilizers in the past twenty years has been very helpful to people in reducing tension without clouding consciousness. Antidepressants and tranquilizers have made it possible for therapists to interact constructively with patients when, without them, the patient would be too uncommunicative, hostile, or excited to profit from such interaction. In certain severe cases, a series of shock treatments may be given, the shock being induced by passage of brief electric current through the brain. In some other severe cases a brain operation may be performed, in which the prefrontal lobes are disconnected from the rest of the brain, though this operation is infrequently performed today. *Psychosurgery*, any surgical intervention in the brain in an attempt to modify behavior, is rare.

Psychological Approaches. In a number of cases it is found that the patient cannot follow directive advice, but that he may be able to work out his own solution to his problems in a series of therapeutic interviews. A number of psychological techniques take this approach. The principal psychological approaches to treatment are outlined below.

Psychoanalysis. In psychoanalysis, the technique of free association is used, in which the patient is to speak whatever comes to his mind however irrelevant or undesirable it may seem. From time to time the patient is given interpretations of the unconscious meaning to him of this material, the interpretations being based on the psychoanalytic theories of personality. There is often noticed a phenomenon called resistance, a temporary or permanent refusal to accept this or other aspects of the psychoanalytic treatment. The aim of the psychoanalytic procedure is not merely to explain the individual's unconscious conflicts to him, for it has often been reported that a patient is not helped if he only accepts these explanations as being plausible. They must also be emotionally accepted before the patient can deal with his conflicts effectively. Psychoanalysis is often a long and costly process.

Non-Directive Therapy (also Called Client-Centered Therapy). In this type of therapy there is no interpretation or instruction, the aim being simply to provide in the therapeutic interviews a sympathetic, non-evaluative atmosphere in which the individual can develop, at his own speed and in his own way, means of dealing with his difficulties. The non-directive system of therapy, though not unique in this aim, is distinguished by the belief that in such an atmosphere the individual will work out his own cure, without diagnosis or specific treatment of his particular type of disorder.

Encounter Groups. The group-therapy format is extended and refined in encounter groups in an attempt to provide each participant with some perspective on how he relates to others in groups. The group usually meets for a single very long session or weekly sessions for a number of weeks. Group members gradually become more candid and less inhibited with one another and thereby provide each other with information about how they relate to others. Reasons for these ways of relating are discussed. Care is taken to ensure that each group member has some say in the way in which the group conducts itself; the group is not to rely on a single leader. Encounter groups are generally thought to be more valuable as short-term learning experiences in human relations than as a psychotherapeutic procedure resulting in enduring personality modifications. As in any type of medical or psychological therapy, one must exercise care in choosing an encounter-group leader in order to be assured that the group will be competently supervised.

Behavior Modification Therapy. Behavior modification therapy places little emphasis on learning about unconscious motives or conflicts that cause problem behavior. Instead, it focuses on the behavior itself. The principles of operant conditioning (see Chapter 3) are used by the therapist to extinguish or alter the expression of the behavior. Behavior modification therapy holds that problem behaviors are learned, and that the application of the principles of learning theory will facilitate the unlearning of these behaviors. Through the process of successive approximation, individuals can be systematically desensitized to the fear they may have of specific objects or situations. By controlling the amount and schedule of various reinforcements, the therapist can extinguish certain behaviors and reward others in their place. Behavior modification techniques are successfully employed in such diverse cases as simple misbehavior in the classroom and bedwetting.

Spontaneous Remission. For reasons which are as yet not fully understood, a number of individuals suffering from personality disorders get well without any special treatment.

PERSONALITY ASSESSMENT

Personality may be assessed in a variety of situations, but formal testing of personality usually involves either questionnaires or the so-called projective tests.

Personality Questionnaires (also called Personality Inventories). Personality questionnaires are similar to vocational interest tests insofar as both are self-report forms on which the individual indicates his answers to questions about himself. The particular questions chosen for inclusion in the test have been empirically tested, and are included because persons with different sorts of personality tend to answer them differently. Most personality inventories assess a number of different personality traits at the same time, providing a separate score for each one. These scores are represented on a graph with a separate scale for each personality trait. When these scores are connected with a line, the resultant curve is called a *personality profile*. It is thought that the characteristics of this profile, its "ups and downs," are more important in personality assessment than any single score for a specific trait. Because an individual answering questions about himself might be less than truthful, some personality inventories include questions intended to detect falsification. In view of the nature and importance of personality profiles, the individual taking them is assured that his scores

Fig. 18. An Example of a Rorschach-Like Inkblot

will be kept confidential and used only for counseling purposes, although abuses of personality inventories are not uncommon.

Projective Tests.   Another way of assessing personality is by using projective tests. These tests typically allow the individual being tested a much greater variety of possible responses than inventories do. This characteristic is well illustrated by the Rorschach Test and the Thematic Apperception Test (TAT), the two most frequently used projective tests. The *Rorschach Test* consists of large ink blots, which are shown to the individual one at a time. He is asked to describe what each looks like to him. The variety of responses possible is very great, just as people differ in seeing shapes of faces or animals or other objects in fleecy summer clouds.

The *Thematic Apperception Test* consists of a number of pictures such as might illustrate magazine stories. The individual makes up a story to go with each picture, thus being permitted a great number of possible responses to the test.

The rationale of a projective test is that, since the stimuli and instructions are the same for all those tested, differences in the way they respond must reflect differences in the people tested, and the test requirements should permit as much as possible of these individual variations to appear. Because of this flexibility, interpretation of the results of projective tests places heavy demands on the skill and judgment of those administering them.

Chapter 11

Social Psychology

SOCIAL ORGANIZATION

It is difficult to study man's psychological characteristics without examining the various groups of which he is a member: his family, his co-workers, his friends. *Social psychology* is the study of the effects of group membership on behavior. People do not live alone; we are all members of *groups* to which we contribute something. Many different types of people may belong to a group, and a group will have an identity of its own apart from the characteristics of the people that compose it. Members of groups influence and change each other, and for this reason groups themselves change and grow. A *society* is made up of a number of groups that are more or less closely related to each other.

Culture. As used in social psychology and anthropology, *culture* means a society's attitudes and beliefs, customs, and traditions. The many groups that comprise a culture typically have similar goals. The goals of a culture's groups give us some idea of the culture's identity. Because most of us have grown up in only one culture, we are likely to underestimate the psychological differences between ourselves and those who have been reared in different cultures. The term *ethnocentrism* refers to feelings of dislike and intolerance for other groups and cultures, and a conviction that one's own group or culture is better than all others. Viewing other cultures from the perspective of one's own reflects both intolerance and prejudice. Social anthropologists who have studied cultures other than ours report kinds of behavior which seem natural to those in the other culture but strange to us. For instance, in the Tchambuli society of New Guinea, it was thought to be natural for women to be dominant, self-sufficient, and dependable, and for men to be sensitive, temperamental, and vain. Various cultures differ in respect to competitiveness, some cultures being much more competitive than that in the United States, and some much less so. Child-rearing practices may vary greatly from one society to another, with each culture regarding its own methods as the best.

Another important cultural issue concerns the distinction between urban and rural lifestyles. The urban lifestyle is dependent upon modern technological advances in the form of better housing and more efficient transportation. Population density is high; the characteristics of buildings and their proximity to one another are very different from the rural environment. The rural lifestyle is not as dependent upon modern advances in housing and transportation; population density is sparse. Social groups in urban and rural settings often are widely different in attitudes, beliefs, customs, traditions, and political ideology. It is therefore likely that urban and rural lifestyles represent different subcultures within a society.

Although various societies differ from each other in many ways, they have in common the phenomenon of social structure.

Social Structure.   In any society different people do different things and interact with different people in various groups. This results in the characteristics of social structure known as position, role, and social class. These characteristics are important to people working in groups because they let the individual know exactly where he stands and outline the nature of his responsibilities. These characteristics are important to the group because they outline the chain of command and designate appropriate channels of communication for group members.

Position, Status.   (These terms in reference to social structure do not mean prestige; see "Social Class" below.) Position is the function one serves in a society: carpenter, mother, witchdoctor, and so forth. Sometimes the positions open to an individual are limited by factors over which he has no control. These are called *ascribed positions*, and include positions, varying from society to society, which are only open to individuals of a specified age or sex, or even to individuals descended from specific individuals. For example, in the United States one may be excluded from the presidency because of age, or one may be forced to retire from a job because of a company's retirement-age policy. In this country, females are not eligible to become combat soldiers, although this is not the case in Israel. In England, one has a chance of becoming king only if his father or uncle was king or his mother was queen by direct inheritance. Many positions, of course, may be obtained by one's skill, expertise, or accomplishments; these are called *achieved positions*. Sometimes one's position results from happenstance, such as marrying the boss's daughter.

The psychological importance of status is that a position is always associated with a role.

Role. Role, by analogy with its theatrical usage, refers to the behavior expected of one in a given position. For instance, a physician is expected to behave calmly, authoritatively, and ethically. A television star is expected to express affection, not contempt, for his audience. A baseball player may endorse a breakfast food; a bank president may not.

In many societies, male and female roles differ in a number of ways. In our society the husband has traditionally been expected to be the principal breadwinner; he is expected to cry seldom, if ever; he is more likely than his wife to hold political office; and so on. In certain other societies, however, these attributes have been characteristic of the female role.

The rather standard roles corresponding to positions have the advantage of making social relations easier. First, they help people to know what to expect of each other. By observing an individual's behavior, others learn to expect similar behavior in the future. Roles are often assigned on the basis of only a minute sample of an individual's total behavioral repertoire. People have a great number of behaviors in common, but by acquiring roles, seemingly small differences are accentuated. Second, the individual, in choosing his own position, knows, at least approximately, what behavior will be expected of him. Since people like to know what to expect from each other, they are likely to apply social pressure toward conformity to those who deviate too much from their roles.

There are also some disadvantages to roles. First, a particular role may not suit an individual, and he must then decide to what extent he should conform to it anyway. Second, one may find himself in a conflict of roles, because each individual frequently has many roles. A woman may need to know the roles appropriate to the positions of wife, mother, citizen, gracious hostess, daughter, first-aid expert, skiing companion, group chairman, part-time secretary, and even more, and be expected to play all these roles successfully at the appropriate times without ever becoming confused. Even if she manages all this, there may be times when two of these roles come into conflict. For instance, suppose that her father insists that her little boy should be forced to wade into the ocean to overcome his fear of it. Her role as mother demands that she protect her boy against what she is sure is dangerous nonsense, but her role as daughter has always involved respect and deference to her father. The two roles are in conflict.

Role conflict can also result from a change in position, as when an enlisted man in the armed forces becomes an officer. Many of his friends are still enlisted men, and when he meets them again he finds that in some ways the role of buddy and the role of officer are incompatible.

It should also be noted that occasionally we acquire a role because of our personality characteristics, and not any special ability or skill. If an individual is thorough, efficient, accepting of other viewpoints, and independent in his thinking, he is likely to be singled out as a leader by his peers. And an authoritarian individual is sometimes assigned a leadership role, even if he doesn't always get along with people.

Social Class. Social class refers to one's prestige level in a society. One basic characteristic of human groups is that there are easily recognizable layers in them, as people tend to separate themselves from one another according to a number of unwritten criteria. The distinctions are more pronounced in some societies than in others. People in a society are well aware of these distinctions in their society, and when asked can readily assign people they know to their positions on the prestige scale. A good deal of enmity often accompanies peoples' judgments concerning the characteristics of, or individuals in, social classes other than their own. Although the names they apply to the various classes may differ (some may call a certain class the "working class," while others may call it the "lower class"), they agree quite well in their ranking of the classes and in the assignment of those they know to these classes.

Class Distinctions.   In the United States, several objective characteristics have been found to differentiate among the social classes:

1) Occupation.

2) Amount of income. This factor can be considerably modified by the source of this income.

3) Source of income. Investment income brings more prestige than income from salary, and income from a salary brings more prestige than hourly wages.

4) Amount of education.

5) Type of home. This includes the area in which it is located.

As an illustrative example, there is presented below the social class structure which was found in one city.

Social Class	*Membership*
lower lower	menial workers and vagrants
upper lower	semi-skilled and unskilled workers
lower middle	white collar and small tradesmen
upper middle	management and owners and upper professional occupations
lower upper	on the average the wealthiest class, the family's wealth having been acquired in the last generation or two
upper upper	wealth has been in the family for several generations and the family has been in this class for several generations, though the average wealth in this class is not as great as it is in the class below it.

One contemporary theorist, Theron Alexander, has suggested that the American culture may be moving away from the type of class distinctions noted above based primarily on occupation and wealth. It has been suggested that we might be moving toward a two-class society based primarily on occupation, family dynamics, and geographical mobility.

The first group includes the working-class family; occupations of individuals in this group range from the semi-skilled worker to the small tradesman. The family structure is typically authoritarian, and the family displays a strong ethnic heritage. Most individuals finish secondary school and few go to college. It is not uncommon for an individual to live in the same neighborhood his entire life. These people have a here-and-now orientation in their lifestyles and seldom plan for the future.

The other group includes mostly professional people. Occupations of individuals in this group include management, owners, upper professionals, and frequently educators. Family structure is notably democratic, without an obvious ethnic identity, and without the degree of cohesiveness seen in the working-class family; divorce is common. Most of these individuals have finished college and many have had extensive postgraduate training. The family is highly mobile, seldom living in one place for more than 5 to 7 years. Individuals of this particular class have a future-oriented lifestyle.

Whether this scheme of social stratification or the previous one is more accurate is hard to say. Both notions have their merits, and each perspective is only useful so long as it poses good questions, summarizes existing knowledge, and predicts future social-group characteristics.

Social Mobility. One obvious implication of a society with a number of social classes and differential prestige accorded to each is that people want to move up to a social class with more prestige than the one in which they were born and raised. This movement from one social class to another (both upward and downward) is called *social mobility.* Upward social mobility is part of the American dream; individuals from the lower social classes are told (and can see) that in our democratic society one can go from rags to riches through his own efforts. It is known that both upward and downward social mobility may cause psychological difficulties; in moving from one social class to another, one is expected to change his lifestyle, whether or not he wants to. When one moves up in society, one moves to a different part of town and makes new acquaintances, often discarding old ones at the same time. There are new social customs to learn. Also, when one achieves a higher social status, he frequently worries about whether he will be able to maintain it. Due to these changes and pressures, signs of maladjustment are common in individuals who experience upward social mobility. Downward social mobility may also require one to change his residence and make new acquaintances, while perhaps being snubbed by the old ones. Downward social mobility is very frustrating.

Even though one's efforts and achievements determine one's social class to a large extent, other factors tend to block social advancement. These include one's race, ethnic origin, religion, and sex.

Psychological Results of Social Class Membership. Members of different social classes tend to differ in several respects. Group pressures to conform to class-specific lifestyles are strong. Some of the ways in which members of various social classes differ include:

1) The amount and kind of magazines, books, and newspapers they read, and the amount and kind of radio-listening, television-watching, and movie-viewing. As a result, views of the world tend to differ from class to class.

2) Their religious memberships, beliefs, and practices.

3) Their political and economic attitudes and buying practices.

4) Their child-rearing practices. (For instance, the lower-class child receives less supervision and more physical punishment.)

5) Their choice of marriage partners. People tend to marry at or close to their own class level.

6) Their ideas of what is correct and proper behavior.

7) The amount and kind of leisure-time activities.

SOCIALIZATION

Socialization means that the individual recognizes his social group's values and beliefs and outlook on the world, and makes them his own. The individual learns to feel comfortable with his group's expectations. The socialization process is extremely complex. When one is fully socialized he experiences little doubt about how to conduct himself when faced with ways of behaving not approved by his culture. It should be pointed out that the socialization process does not ensure the individual's psychological growth, as many of our society's expectations do not foster the free expression of our motives or our desire to pursue our individual interests while deferring our responsibilities. The process of socialization begins soon after birth, and the child is faced with many years of social learning. Some important aspects of early socialization include dependency, acquiring values, impulse control, delay of gratification, and identification.

Dependency. The infant and young child are totally dedependent upon those who take care of them for nutrition, affection, and sensory stimulation. Later, the child learns facts and strategies for coping with uncertainty, and these also reflect the influence of his "caretakers." In other words, the parent commonly handles all early socialization experiences. The child's style of reliance on others to meet his needs is thus established early in life.

Values. The child learns when very young to attribute different degrees of importance or desirability to things, ideas, or people. This is what we mean by a *value*. Values have the characteristics of acquired motives (see Chapter 5). While young, the child is rewarded for behavior representative of the parents' values, and so his earliest values are those of his parents. Later, the individual keeps or discards parental values as he sees fit. Through the process of socialization the individual learns to reward himself for behavior in keeping with his own values. In this way, the individual acquires a capacity for self-control.

Impulse Control. While culture sanctions the acquisition of some values, others that threaten group cohesiveness are suppressed. In the course of socialization, the child learns, through punishment that others dispense, those behaviors considered appropriate. Through this experience, the child learns to inhibit some of his behavior, and he internalizes other behavior. As the child gradually makes society's values his own, he is better able to recognize and control impulses that have led to punishment in the past. By controlling his impulses the child indicates that he understands the potential consequences of his behavior. As was pointed out in Chapter 3, punishment here serves to suppress undesirable behavior in order to permit the occurrence of desirable behavior that can be rewarded.

Delay of Gratification. Socialization involves learning to suppress a socially unacceptable desire for immediate rewards in order to receive rewards at a later time that are of greater value to the individual and his society. Individuals thus learn to work toward long-range goals of lasting importance.

Identification. As was noted in Chapter 10, a child learns the attitudes and values of his society through a process of identification with some significant adult, usually the same-sex parent. Behaviors appropriate to one's sex-role are learned in this way, and uncertainty concerning socially acceptable behavior is resolved. The child presumably receives rewards from his parents for identifying with them. These rewards may generalize to his relationships with others.

Problems in Socialization.   Not all children and adolescents go through the socialization process completely or with equal ease. The characteristics of modern urban society emphasize depersonalized lifestyles. For this reason, many have difficulty fitting into social groups. Many feel left out. We often say that these individuals are *alienated*. These individuals have difficulty earning a livelihood and accepting family values and responsibilities. They often feel that they are remote from the product of their labor and the process of their society. They are frequently unsuccessful in their educational and vocational endeavors, and therefore find themselves without occupational choices and with substandard salaries.

In the course of socialization, the individual recognizes that a culture's primary rewards are derived through participation in the occupational system. These rewards include financial security, prestige, and a sense of accomplishment and productivity. However, a youth is often limited to insignificant participation in the occupational system. He is not paid what his labor is worth because he is young. Thus, early in life an individual may be denied the fundamental rewards of job satisfaction.

Our society is success-oriented and emphasizes the need to achieve and succeed as a way of life. Yet some individuals, because of their social status or race, will face a large number of seemingly insurmountable obstacles in their attempts to succeed. Also, if an individual's skills and interests do not fit the immediate needs of his society he may become frustrated.

The alienated individual often behaves apathetically. He may feel lost in society. He frequently experiences poverty and may express his frustration in the form of delinquency. Alienation thus involves large numbers of people who do not recognize the norms of their society as their own.

BEHAVIOR IN SMALL GROUPS

Much valuable information about social structure has come from the study of small groups, which are in some ways miniature societies. The trend in research on small-group behavior has been toward quantitative and experimental study of the kinds of interaction occurring in groups, the effects of group structure, and how leadership affects group activities.

Factors Affecting Group Performance.   Are two or more heads better than one? The answer to this question depends upon several factors. In general, however, when a number of individuals pool their talents and resources, their efforts are likely to be more effective than an individual working alone. We will now discuss several important factors concerning group performance.

Complexity of Problem. When a problem can be divided into small parts or when problems deal with single, simple issues, a group can accomplish more than a number of people working alone.

Relations between Group Members. When a group works on a problem that requires the collection of a large amount of information, a core of a few group members tends to gather and evaluate the information efficiently. However, when a group works on a complex problem, group members would do well to divide up into smaller, less-centralized groups and attempt a number of solutions independent of each other at the same time. It should also be pointed out that while somewhat larger groups have more people contributing their skills to the solution of a problem, the greater the number of people, the more opportunity there is for conflicts to develop.

Group Members' Values. People who are somewhat alike in their values work better together than those holding conflicting values. Groups will not function harmoniously or productively if individual members have different motives for participating and different goals in mind.

Leadership in Small Groups. Various individual differences are seen among leaders of small groups. These differences can have important effects on the development of group success. Generally they may be characterized in the following ways.

Personal Characteristics of Leaders. In one type of experimental research on leadership, small groups with problems to solve have, without knowing that they were in an experiment, been given leaders with different characteristics for the purpose of comparison. In working on its first problem, a group might have a leader who was very unpleasant but very capable at the task. The leader for the second problem might be quite likeable but not very useful. Given a choice of leaders for the third problem, the group members were likely to prefer the capable though disagreeable leader.

Leadership is not a general characteristic of an individual. Instead, it results from the interaction of the individual's abilities and characteristics with those which the specific situation requires of a leader. Also of importance are the structure of the group, the kind of problem, and the values of the group members. Should the problem with which a group is confronted change, so might the group's leader.

Group Structure. Another factor affecting leadership is the structure of the group, that is, who can communicate with whom. For instance, suppose that a group is so structured that there is one central individual to whom all others in the group report, while being unable to communicate with each other. Only the central individual is in a position to receive all the information available to the group and to coordinate the group's activities. Almost automatically any individual in this central position will become the leader of the group. At the other extreme, suppose there is a group in which all members can communicate freely with each other. No position of leadership is imposed by the group structure.

Leadership Strategies. Experiments were carried out on several clubs of ten-year-old boys to see what effects several kinds of leadership would have. There were three types of leadership:

1) Authoritarian. The leader made all decisions and monitored the boys' activities.

2) Laissez-Faire. The leader did very little more than speak when spoken to.

3) Democratic. Decisions about group activities were made by the group, with the leader serving as group discussion leader. He also participated to some extent in the activities.

These different kinds of leadership had these different kinds of results:

1) Democratic. The boys were friendly with each other and with their leader; there was some horseplay; there was reasonably satisfactory output.

2) Laissez-Faire. This group spent the least time in constructive work, the most time in horseplay; they were discontented.

3) Authoritarian. There were two kinds of reaction to authoritarian leadership: passive and aggressive.

In the passive-reaction groups, most of the time was spent in work, with little talk, either friendly or unfriendly. Later, when these boys were transferred to democratic leadership, there was at first much aggression released.

In the aggressive-reaction groups, there was aggressive behavior and picking on a scapegoat; the output equaled the democratic group, but the work was disrupted if the leader left.

Group leaders have also been categorized as people-centered and task-centered. The *people-centered leader* is sensitive to the attitudes, motivation, and capability of those working under him. The *task-centered leader* is concerned with getting the job done and is less aware of the individual characteristics of those working under him. It has been found that these styles of leadership are more or less efficient depending on the nature of the situation. When a situation is either very good or very bad the task-oriented leader is more efficient. When a situation is somewhat good without any major difficulties the person-oriented leader is more efficient.

Group Pressure. It is readily apparent that groups attempt to bring about what they regard as sufficient conformity by their members through the use of instruction, example, and reward and punishment. The experiment below illustrates group pressure in the absence of these methods.

In this experiment, each subject believed that he was one of a group of subjects who were making simple perceptual judgments. Actually, all of the other "subjects" were accomplices of the experimenter, and before the start of the experiment were instructed what judgments to make.

Judging Line Length. The stimuli in this experiment were not at all ambiguous. Members of the group were required to give their estimates of the lengths of lines drawn on white cards. If all the accomplices' estimates were quite close to each other and quite different from those of the subject, about one-quarter of the subject's judgments were unaffected while the rest of the subjects changed their judgments to some degree. (Often there was some rationalization involved, such as the possibility of unsuspected eye difficulty.)

It was found that increasing beyond four the number of those disagreeing with the subject had little additional effect; it was also found that if only one accomplice gave estimates in good agreement with those of the subject, the efforts of the group pressure were greatly decreased.

What Are the Causes of Conformity? People typically conform to group pressures for a wide variety of reasons. Conformity to group norms makes it possible for an individual to avoid being labeled as deviant. It also allows the individual to entrust his social group with the job of defining and maintaining expectations of his behavior; he won't have to think for himself.

This gives the individual some anonymity and allows him to dilute his own responsibility for certain behaviors because the group now assumes those responsibilities. Conformity is enhanced because groups punish nonconformist behavior.

Personal Space. Another important factor concerning the behavior of individuals in groups is *personal space*, or the physical distance people keep between each other. In our interaction with others, there is a space around ourselves that we would like others to stay out of; it can be a foot or two or several feet. Several factors determine the size of an individual's personal space in various situations. When we know someone fairly well we do not mind being close to him, but we keep our distance with strangers. Also, different cultural norms contribute to our ideas about proximity to others, and these vary from one society to another.

The space people keep between each other can facilitate or hinder group performance. When group members must cooperate in order to perform efficiently, they are more likely to work well when close together.

ATTITUDES AND BELIEFS IN SOCIAL GROUPS

Attitude and Belief Defined. An *attitude* is a predisposition to react favorably or unfavorably toward someone or something. A *belief* is an idea that one thinks is true, and it is one important component of an attitude. Our feelings and actions are also part of our attitudes.

Prejudice. As the term is used in social psychology, *prejudice* refers to an attitude that predisposes us to think about people, objects, or cultural groups in a set way, and not to change our thinking when we learn new information about these people, objects, or cultural groups. Prejudice also refers to reactions to others based on their group membership rather than on their individual characteristics. We form our attitudes through personal experience, but the role of our parents' attitudes, our peer-groups, and the mass media are also very important. Some of these will be discussed later. Also, the role of our emotions cannot be discounted in the formation of prejudiced attitudes. The groups that are frequently the object of prejudiced attitudes in turn have their own prejudices against those segments of society that discriminate against them. This is called *reverse prejudice*.

Stereotypes. In social psychology a *stereotype* is a set of beliefs, not always accurate and often overgeneralized, about the characteristics thought to be shared by most members of a particular group. For instance, people from the Mediterranean area are supposed by many to be impulsive and artistic, while the people of northern Europe are held by some to be calm and industrious. South Sea islanders, on the other hand, are frequently characterized as easygoing and unambitious. Even as broad generalizations, stereotypes have only very limited validity; and on an individual basis, stereotypes are virtually meaningless. Many individuals in any group will be found to have traits which the stereotype uses to characterize other groups.

Development of Attitudes and Beliefs. Attitudes and beliefs may be determined by a number of factors, some of which are discussed here:

Personal Experience. One's attitudes can be a result of one's own experience, perhaps a single dramatic instance, or a series of consistent happenings. This is not always the case, however. Over many decades, college students have expressed consistent prejudices about the nationalities of those whom they would or would not like to have as fellow-workers, neighbors, members of the family, and so forth. In many cases, they had never encountered any representatives of these nationalities, but this did not prevent their having attitudes toward them.

The Examples and Teachings of Others. When the development of prejudices in children is observed, it is often found that their attitudes toward other groups have developed before any corresponding stereotypes or reasons appear. Apparently the generalized attitude is acquired or implanted first, and only later are the details filled in. In view of the remarks made earlier in this chapter concerning the role of identification in socialization, it is likely that attitudes and beliefs are acquired through this process.

Information. Since the information transmitted to us by others is of necessity selected, we may develop attitudes different from those we would have if all the details of a given situation were made available to us, rather than merely those that our informant is aware of or cares to pass on to us.

Type of Personality. There has been some research indicating that persons with an "authoritarian" personality are more likely to be ethnocentric and hostile toward other groups. The authoritarian individual is thought to project his own inadequacies onto cultural groups other than his own.

Maintenance of Attitudes and Beliefs. Since we are often exposed to situations and to information which may conflict with our attitudes and stereotypes, we may ask why attitudes are nevertheless so often firmly held.

Selective Perception and Remembering. It has been shown that one is more likely to remember information which favors the attitudes he holds, and more likely not to remember information which disagrees with those attitudes. While it is not yet clear how much of this effect results from selective perception, and how much from selective remembering, the net effect is the same.

Self-Screening. One is likely to withdraw from information which contradicts his own attitudes. He may turn off the radio or television, throw down the magazine or book, or walk out on a speaker when views are expressed which disagree strongly with his own. Thereby he avoids much of the effect which these presentations might otherwise have on him. Conversely, he may seek out information which agrees with his attitudes.

Social Reward and Punishment. When most of a group have similar attitudes about something, those who express agreement win approval, while those who disagree can expect disapproval. History records many instances in which social punishment of attitudes has extended beyond disapproval to economic reprisal, expulsion, or death. Social rewards and punishments directly affect only the expression of attitudes, rather than the attitudes themselves. However, the effect is often the same—many choose to behave as if their attitudes were those of the group.

Dissonance. The concept of dissonance, in relation to attitudes, refers to an inconsistency one perceives between his attitudes or beliefs and his behavior, such as the inconsistency between a belief that smoking is not good for one and the fact that one continues to smoke. Dissonance is psychologically uncomfortable.

The concept can be related to the factors listed above which help to maintain attitudes and beliefs. One can minimize dissonance by forgetting or avoiding anything which contradicts one's attitudes. In the face of social pressure to change one's attitudes, if one conforms, he can reduce the importance of the resulting dissonance by a suitable rationalization.

In addition, one may reduce dissonance by changing his beliefs, adding new ones, or changing his behavior.

Propaganda and Attitude Change. Much time and effort is spent in the effort to change beliefs and attitudes. Individuals, advertisers, politicians, and nations are all at one time or another interested in producing attitude change. Although the word "propaganda" is often used with the approximate meaning of "the lies the other side tells," in social psychology it means merely any communication intended to affect attitudes and opinions. Those who propagandize do not engage in a logical give-and-take of different viewpoints; there is really no dispute. The propagandist understands the solution to his argument before he states it. Propaganda takes account of popular sentiment and discourages the scrutiny of observable, measurable facts. The propagandist is successful if he tailors his message to the social and personality characteristics of his audience. There are several commonly used propaganda techniques which have an important bearing on attitude change:

1) *Stereotyping.* Propagandists overgeneralize the characteristics of various social groups, exaggerate their negative qualities, and make it difficult to form and maintain independent attitudes and opinions. Societies then perpetuate these negative stereotypes.

2) *Repetition.* The propagandist's message is frequently repeated, often in several different media. Slogans and jingles are widely broadcast. It is important to note that the content of the message is seldom critically evaluated; we don't think about what we are repeating.

3) *Scapegoating.* The propagandist often presents a double message; he states his thoughts not only in favor of something, but also against something else. The propagandist may blame many social problems which affect most of the society's citizens on a single, easily recognizable cultural group. Public sentiment as well as the media may then align themselves against this group.

4) *Characteristics of the Source.* It is not surprising that propaganda tends to be more effective if it comes from a source in whom one has confidence. For this reason, the appeal of the

propagandist is often made on the basis of the fact that authoritative segments of society have accepted his thinking, or that a major share of the society has accepted it.

5) *Fear.* There have been experiments which show that propaganda which attempts to achieve its aim by frightening people is not very effective. Apparently such propaganda is self-destructive, for if it does succeed in frightening people the distress they experience causes them to forget the propaganda itself.

THE SELF IN SOCIAL INTERACTION

The Nature of the Self. The *self* is what we see when we look at ourselves from various perspectives without using a mirror. It is a cluster of our psychological qualities and predispositions; we can think of our selves in many ways. The self is thought of in terms of our own characteristics when we view ourselves in isolation, and also when we compare ourselves to others. The concept of the self develops through learning, when we are children and note the reactions of others to us and our behavior; through the rewards and punishments from others our values and attitudes are formed. Although we adopt various roles as the situation demands, the self is a fairly enduring and consistent, yet flexible, attribute. The self-concept involves egocentric behavior; while as adults we are capable of viewing objects, people, or events from the perspective of others, we still feel that we are the center of things. The self-concept is not necessarily reality-oriented, but even though our perceptions of ourselves may not be wholly accurate, they are the perceptions that we use in our day-to-day behavior. We shall now view the nature of the self from various perspectives.

The Social Setting. We typically accommodate our behavior to the demands of different social situations, playing one of various roles as the setting dictates. The values and attitudes of our social groups determine the way in which we view ourselves. The influence of the expectations of others in our formulating our self-concept is great. Because all of us have a desire to be unique in some respects, we often compare ourselves to others in social settings in order to determine the degree to which we are different or similar to other group members.

The Ideal Self. We frequently compare the person we perceive ourselves to be with the person we would like to be, our *ideal self.* When it looks as though the perceived self approximates the ideal self or when it looks as though we are well on the way to realizing the ideal self, we have feelings of adequacy and high self-esteem. We typically feel inadequate if our perceived selves and ideal selves are too different from each other.

Possessions and Self-Image. People often define their self-concepts in terms of the possessions that they own. The car one drives, the home one owns and the part of town in which it is located, one's home furnishings, and accomplishments with some tangible financial meaning (a college degree, for example) are part of one's self-concept. Self-esteem is frequently related to the quantity and quality of one's possessions. People therefore are often concerned with the display of these objects; they equate them with signs of their accomplishments.

Self-Disclosure. It has been suggested that we only really get to know ourselves by describing ourselves in words, out loud, to others. This has obvious implications for personality growth, however it is also important to the nature of our working relationships with others. Real self-disclosure is rare and depends on a few important factors: the nature of the relationship with the individual to whom one is speaking, and the part of one's personality one is describing. It has been learned that individuals listening to others disclosing information about themselves frequently reciprocate. Some types of personal information are easier to disclose than other types. As people become more intimate with each other, they disclose more of themselves.

ATTRIBUTING CHARACTERISTICS TO OTHERS

Evaluating Others. In our dealings with other people, we are often curious to know whether their behavior toward us is truly representative of their personality or if they are trying to project a certain image, or make a certain impression. For this reason, our evaluation of others' behavior often involves some thought about their underlying motives. We react to others on the basis of the way in which we perceive them. Because a true understanding of another's motives for behaving in a certain way is difficult to gain, we frequently behave toward others on the basis of motives and characteristics *we* attribute to them. These attributions are based on the consistency with which others behave in a variety of situations, our preconceived notions about them, the degree to which others agree with our appraisals, and our estimation of how free others are to behave as they really are. Each of these will be discussed in an attempt to better understand the attribution process.

Consistency in the Behavior of Others.   We become more and more sure that the characteristics we attribute to others are real when we observe some consistency in the expression of these characteristics in their behavior. We know a good deal about an individual when we can recognize the consistencies in his behavior in various situations.

Preconceived Notions about the Behavior of Others.   We commonly attribute characteristics to others that we expect them to have on the basis of their membership in various social groups or because of stereotypes we might hold. It is also common to attribute characteristics to someone whom we have not yet met on the basis of information provided us by others.

Our Attribution Depends on Others' Attribution.   We seldom attribute characteristics to another individual without first checking to see if others attribute the same characteristics to him. In a sense, our attributions are reinforced by others. We look to others to reconfirm our judgments.

Pressures to Conform.   In attributing characteristics to others on the basis of observable behavior, we must ask ourselves whether or not the individual is behaving as he would really like to. Social pressures to conform might encourage him to behave in a way that is not really "him." Our attributions would therefore not be accurate.

ATTRACTION

Social psychologists are interested in the factors that bring and hold people together. *Attraction* is a topic of relevance to group performance, interpersonal relationships, the self-concept, and the qualities we attribute to others. When others have attitudes and personality traits that we think are important, we are often attracted to them. Beauty, ability, and an open rapport are all meaningful aspects of attraction between people. Several factors in attraction will now be discussed.

Similarity.   People enjoy social interaction with those much like themselves; common interests are very important in the attraction between people. Age, occupation, and socioeconomic status are among those factors important in attractions.

Proximity.   Being physically close to others or having the opportunity to get close to others is an important factor in interpersonal attraction. People are more likely to become friends with those next door than those down the street. However, it should be remembered in connection with our earlier remarks about personal space that proximity *per se* does not ensure interpersonal attraction, and that violation of one's personal space can actually cause interpersonal tension.

Complementarity.   When two individuals recognize that their interests and abilities are different, they may see that their interests and abilities complement each other's, that one's abilities make up for the other's deficiencies. While complementarity is not always a sufficiently meaningful part of the attraction between two people to enhance a long-lasting relationship, in some cases it is very important.

Esteem.   Even though some individuals are dissimilar from us, are not physically close to us, and do not have attitudes or abilities which complement our own, we still feel some attraction for them on the basis of their highly respected personality characteristics. For instance, we often feel an attraction for those who are intelligent, industrious, articulate, sincere, honest, and have integrity.

This chapter has described that portion of psychology which is customarily referred to as social psychology, but much of the rest of this book is also significant for social psychology. Man's social interactions are affected by his motives, experience, and personality, by his abilities and beliefs, and by the biological factors which may influence them. In turn, his social environment has profound effects upon his psychological characteristics. No aspect of man's nature can be regarded as wholly irrelevant to any other aspect, and it is only by trying to understand all aspects of man that we can even hope to understand him completely.

Chapter 12

Psychology: History, Methods, and Goals

THE FIELD OF PSYCHOLOGY

Psychology Defined. As the past chapters have shown, psychology is the study of behavior, both of human beings and of animals. The basic source of psychological knowledge is the observable activities of organisms. But the province of the psychologist also includes such concepts as emotion, learning, unconscious motivation, and personality, our knowledge of which is inferred from overt behavior, rather than being directly observed. Various subdisciplines of psychology have developed different methods that enhance the accuracy of inferences concerning a great variety of behavior. New techniques of observation are being perfected.

Relation of Psychology to Psychiatry, Psychoanalysis, and Sociology. The terms "psychiatry" and "psychoanalysis" are frequently confused with "psychology." Although related to the general field of psychology, these two terms have special meanings. "Sociology" has its own field, but touches psychology at various points.

Psychiatry is a branch of medicine which deals with mental illness. It is concerned with the study and treatment of mental disorders that disrupt an individual's daily functioning. Less-serious behavior disorders are also dealt with by the psychiatrist and the psychologist with training in counseling techniques.

Another branch of psychology, *clinical psychology*, also concerns the diagnosis and cure of mental illness. However, the clinical psychologist's training is in psychology, not in medicine. Clinical psychologists are particularly well qualified to administer and interpret psychological tests and to conduct psychological research.

Psychoanalysis, as a term, has two closely related meanings. The first meaning of psychoanalysis is the specific theory of personality developed by Sigmund Freud, and the other theories that have derived from Freud's work. The second meaning of psychoanalysis is the method of treating mental and emotional disturbance by the application of psychoanalytic theories.

The close connection between psychology and both psychiatry and psychoanalysis is apparent. Yet it should be kept in mind that psychology includes other specific areas of behavioral study, all of which have been considered in this book.

Sociology concerns the organization and process of people living in groups. While psychology is more concerned with individual behavior, sociology is concerned with the behavior of groups as wholes. *Social psychology*, as we have just seen, deals with the reactions of individuals within groups, but does not study the characteristics of whole groups as sociology does.

A BRIEF HISTORY OF PSYCHOLOGY

The First Psychological Laboratory. Man has long been interested in understanding his fellows, and psychological generalizations have been expressed by such diverse thinkers as Confucius, Socrates, Machiavelli, and Descartes. However, it was not until 1879 that a laboratory in Germany at the University of Leipzig began to produce psychological information by the use of experimental methods. This laboratory was founded by Wilhelm Wundt (1832–1920), a physiologist turned psychologist. Several of the first psychological laboratories in the United States were started by Wundt's students.

Before that time, the few psychological experiments performed were incidental to the work of scientists in other fields. For instance, the first studies of reaction time were begun in 1820 by astronomers who found, when they attempted to measure the time of certain astronomical events to the nearest 1/10th second, that different observers consistently obtained different results, sometimes disagreeing by as much as a whole second. Experimental investigations showed the differences to be the result of individual reaction times. Thus, because of a problem which arose in the course of astronomical research, reaction time experiments, later the concern of psychologists, were first performed by astronomers over half a century before Wundt established his laboratory.

Psychology before the Laboratory Stage. Laboratory psychology did not make its appearance merely because of incidental problems in other scientific fields, however. It was a natural result of trends in philosophy and physiology.

Among the questions of perennial interest to philosophers—from the beginnings of systematic rational thought with the Greeks—were many concerning reasoning, how man acquired knowledge and morals, the association of ideas, and so on. The philosopher Plato believed that our psychological characteristics are inborn and that our experiences play only a minor role. Plato thought that information about the world coming to us through our senses was distorted because our senses are unreliable. Plato took the position that the mind and the body are separate aspects of ourselves and that they do not influence each other. Aristotle, who had studied with Plato, looked at these issues somewhat differently. According to Aristotle, our psychological characteristics are due to the various experiences we have. He thought that the senses function accurately in supplying us with information about our environments. He also felt that the functions of the body and the functions of the mind are related to each other.

The nineteenth-century British philosopher John Locke held the view that the mind's content is determined by experience. Locke wrote about the ways in which ideas seem to relate to one another through the process of association. Locke was also interested in the role of the senses in our accumulation of knowledge. He also felt that when we are born the mind is a *tabula rasa* (blank slate), and that our sensations and experiences are "engraved" on this slate.

It was the practice of these philosophers to try to answer these questions by reasoning based upon common experience rather than upon facts obtained under carefully chosen conditions of observation. When modern philosophy placed its emphasis primarily upon inductive rather than deductive knowledge, it was inevitable that attempts would be made to answer such psychological questions by scientific investigation.

Studying the functioning of organs of the body, physiologists were learning much about the senses, and something about the brain. They found that this led them to questions in the psychology of perception and of thinking. For example, coal in sunlight sends more light to your eye than a piece of chalk in shadow does. Why doesn't the coal look lighter than the chalk? The great physiologist Helmholtz, more than a century ago, proposed to account for this and similar phenomena with his theory of "unconscious inference."

This theory did not involve such conventional physiological concepts as sensory receptors or activity in nerve fibers, but invoked psychological concepts such as learning through experience and subconscious thought. Physiological research was raising psychological questions, for which psychological explanations were being proposed. The work of Müller, Weber, and Fechner referred to in Chapter 7 are examples of this process.

Thus both philosophy and physiology were encountering psychological questions for which factual answers might be expected to result from vigorous research, and Wundt's establishment of his laboratory was the first major step in pursuit of that aim.

Another important influence on the growth of psychology came from the realm of the natural sciences. The writings of Charles Darwin on evolutionary theory and emotion were at the time very controversial, but they suggested that humans, in body form and *perhaps* in mental functioning, were descended from subhuman ancestors. The notion that psychologists can learn something about human psychological functioning by studying animals thus stems from Darwin's writings. Much of the information presented in the chapters concerning emotion, motivation, and learning was first discovered by studying animal behavior, and then attempts were made to find counterparts in human behavior.

Schools of Psychology.   It was all very well to start laboratories of psychology, but it was necessary to decide what to do in them, and also to decide what the task of psychology was to be. In view of the fact that the early psychologists were trained in various traditions, including the philosophical, physiological, and biological, there were many ways of looking upon the subject-matter included in this new discipline. Also, different individuals thought that different methods were appropriate to the study of psychological processes. Consequently, in addition to carrying on their research, many of these pioneers formed schools or movements in psychology, groups with differing beliefs in what psychology should consist of and how it should go about its work.

The following brief descriptions give some idea of various approaches which were advocated.

Structuralism. The analysis of the normal adult human mind was considered by the structuralists to be psychology's task. This was to be accomplished by the method of introspection, by the mind "looking into" itself by the use of standardized techniques. By analogy with the procedures of chemistry, a field in which great advances had been made by analyzing compounds into their constituent elements, the well-trained introspective observer was to analyze his own perceptions, motivations, and feelings, and to discover the mental elements of which they were composed and the laws governing the combination of these elements into psychological compounds. E. B. Titchener (1867–1927), who had studied under Wundt, was the leader of this school in the United States.

This approach presented two problems. First, if two well-trained introspectionists obtained different results, there was no way to decide whether one of them was in error or if the two minds were actually different, since no one else could look into a man's mind to check up on his observations. Second, since introspective psychology could obtain its data only from those who could become trained introspectionists, it excluded the study of child psychology, animal psychology, psychopathology, and other areas in which the subjects could not become skilled introspectionists.

Functionalism. The functionalists took psychology's task to be the study of how mental operations serve the needs of the organism. One was not to analyze mental phenomena into their elements, but to investigate how they functioned in affecting an organism's goals and the achievement of them. Therefore psychology's concerns were to include educational psychology, and learning in animals and men—in short, all the branches of psychology which had been excluded by structuralism.

In its emphasis on the utility of psychological characteristics to the organism, functionalism clearly was influenced by Darwin's theory of evolution, published less than forty years earlier, in 1859. Psychological characteristics, no less than physical characteristics, affect an organism's adaptation to its environment.

The functionalists were still interested in conscious thought processes, and had no objection, for example, to the subject in an experiment on problem solving describing what he thought about as he worked. His report was to be descriptive, however, and not an attempt at the structuralist sort of analysis.

Two American figures who made outstanding contributions to the school of functionalism were William James (1842–1910) and John Dewey (1859–1952).

Behaviorism. The school of behaviorism, founded by the American psychologist John B. Watson (1878–1958), rejected from psychology all data which were not publicly observable, on the grounds that they were not objective and were therefore unscientific. The mind and its conscious processes, being available only to private introspection by the individual, were disregarded by the behaviorists. To the study of man one was, accordingly, to apply objective methods, just as one did in animal psychology in which one never investigated the mind of the mouse or the consciousness of the earthworm. Objective observations of stimuli and response, and the relations among them, was to be the task of psychology.

Though not a necessary consequence of the behaviorist position, there was often, though not always, a tendency to throw out the brain as well as the mind. For instance, it was proposed that thinking consisted only of talking to oneself, the relevant activity in this case consisting solely of tiny movements of the speech mechanism, muscle movements too small to be observed without special devices. Another position held by many behaviorists, although this too was not a necessary consequence of their position, was a strong environmentalism. That is, inborn differences among people were thought to be negligible or nonexistent. Temperament, ability, personality—all were held to be acquired by the building up of great numbers of the conditioned reflexes which were then being studied by the Russian physiologist Ivan Pavlov. These reflexes were described in Chapter 3. The best-known modern behaviorist is B. F. Skinner (1904–   ). In view of the fact that behaviorism is concerned with the behavior elicited by stimuli, it is often called *stimulus-response psychology.*

Gestalt Psychology. Gestalt psychology drew its name because of the insistence by its German originators that *die Gestalt* —the entire configuration—of a psychological phenomenon was different from the sum of its parts. The Gestaltists, among them Max Wertheimer (1880–1943), Kurt Koffka (1886–1941) and Wolfgang Köhler (1887–1967), drew analogies from examples in the physical sciences to support their contention that the result of combining elements could not be predicted merely from knowledge of the properties of the elements, but that the resulting "Gestalt" had properties of its own. Thus they point out that the properties of water are not merely the sum of the properties of the hydrogen and oxygen composing it. Consequently, this movement was strongly opposed to the analytical approach of the structuralists, and to the behavioristic explanations in terms of collections of conditioned responses.

Gestalt psychologists, like functionalists, were interested in descriptions of their subjects' conscious mental processes, when possible, as well as in the study of children and animals. Much of their research was in the fields of perception and memory, to which they made important contributions. They also investigated the phenomenon of *insight*, a type of learning involving an unusually quick grasp of the solution to a problem.

The Gestalt perspective in psychology is currently being applied to several areas of human behavior having little to do with the original investigations. Some of these include dream analysis and group processes.

The Significance of These Schools. It should not be thought from the foregoing descriptions that the early psychologists did nothing but spend their time arguing. Much research was accomplished during these decades. It should also be emphasized that this division into "schools" is largely a thing of the past. Nowadays it would be hard to find many psychologists who would identify themselves exclusively with one or another of these movements.

The reason for reviewing the major schools here is that present-day psychology has been shaped by its past. The structuralist and Gestalt interest in perception are also found in modern psychology; the early radical behaviorism is responsible for the present emphasis on the distinction between objective data and the inferences made from them; the functionalists' interest in practical uses of psychology flourishes on the modern scene; and much current experimentation is specifically designed to assess the complex interactions emphasized by the Gestalt school.

Other Major Influences in Psychology.   Two other major influences on modern psychology have not yet been mentioned here—testing and psychoanalysis. We will discuss them now.

Testing.   Among the earliest contributors to the study of individual differences in ability was Sir Francis Galton (1822–1911), with his studies of the inheritance of genius, and his devising of various tests of human abilities.

Galton's work was an important step in the objective study of psychological differences among individuals, but most of the study of these differences came only after the development of intelligence tests. The development, use and meaning of these tests were discussed in Chapter 9, and the fundamental contributions of Alfred Binet were noted.

Psychoanalysis.   Psychoanalysis is presented here in the first of its two meanings—the theory of personality proposed by Sigmund Freud, rather than his method of treatment. Freud found the then-available theories of neurotic illness quite unsatisfactory; and, on the basis of his own clinical experience, developed the theory of human motivation, personality development, and personality disorders known as psychoanalysis. These theories were outlined in Chapter 10. Although psychoanalysis has been and is controversial, there is now little rejection of Freud's emphasis on the existence of unconscious motives and memories.

The breadth of Freud's theories is shown by the fact that portions of them appeared in this book in various chapters—those covering memory, motivation, and personality. Psychoanalytic theories have influenced not only psychology and psychiatry, but also literature, drama, the arts, and cinema. Although parts of Freud's theories are still disputed, it is probably safe to say that no other psychologist has had as much impact on modern thought as he has had.

Some Recent Trends in Psychology.   Two relatively recent trends in psychology involve the influence of humanistic and cognitive theories concerning human behavior and its development. Both of these views are dissatisfied with the notion that man is a basically irrational animal, subject to the influence of his unconscious sexual and aggressive impulses. These theorists also feel that there is more to our behavior than chains of conditioned responses as the behaviorists maintain.

Humanistic Psychology. Humanistic psychologists believe that we are capable of personality growth as long as we live. We are capable of recognizing our need to grow and of deliberately involving ourselves in experiences that will enhance that growth. These psychologists believe that our needs for feelings of personal fulfillment, accomplishment, worth, and happiness are basic to our daily behavior and motivate many of our actions.

Humanistic theorists encourage us to accept the fact that some unpleasant emotions such as grief and guilt are part of living and should not be hidden and ignored. In attributing importance to continual growth, these psychologists emphasize that our current behavior is the product of our past, but also determines much of our future behavior. The humanistic doctrine maintains that each of us is directly responsible for all of our behavior and that we thereby determine the quality of our own lives.

The humanistic perspective is currently being applied not only as a tool in psychotherapy but also as a vehicle for understanding the adult personality and its development. Its chief proponents include Abraham Maslow (1908–1970) and Carl Rogers (1902–   ).

Cognitive Psychology. Cognitive psychologists are dissatisfied with stimulus-response psychology because it tends to mechanize our reception of stimuli and production of responses, and because in it little emphasis is placed on humans as thinking, evaluating, rational beings. The cognitive theorists hold that we have many innate abilities that help us to act on our surroundings and derive information from them. Intellectual development and language development are two areas widely investigated from the cognitive perspective. Emphasis is placed on our interaction with our environment and our ability to organize that experience into meaningful, useful behavior. In addition to language and intellectual growth, cognitive psychologists have also been interested in human perceptual processes and memory.

METHODS IN PSYCHOLOGY

Limitations of the Common-Sense Approach.   Since each of us has to deal with other people, each of us has acquired some common-sense psychology. We usually feel we have a pretty fair understanding of why people react as they do, and what to expect from them—though they sometimes surprise us. In fact, the opinion is sometimes heard that most of psychology is just "plain common sense."

It was once a matter of plain common sense that the world was flat, which shows that common sense has to be verified. Of course, checking on common sense sometimes shows common sense to be right. It is important, however, to distinguish between being right by accident, and being right because of sound reasoning based on careful observation.

Of course, many common-sense generalizations are based on observation. The difficulty is that too often it is casual observation made under specific conditions, and the conclusions are drawn only from the exceptional, vivid cases which are easily remembered. In all branches of science, it has been found that acquiring sound data requires the application of scientific method.

Characteristics of Scientific Method. Scientific method is essentially a way of investigating nature, a way which has been shown by experience to be helpful in arriving at accurate observations and conclusions. Many of the details of scientific method differ from one discipline to another, but certain general characteristics are common to all.

Objectivity. Disinterested (not uninterested) search for truth. Though scientists often have their preferences among ideas, the ideal requires that neither the preferences and preconceptions of the investigator nor those of anyone else be allowed to influence his research findings.

Lawfulness. The regularity and consistency of nature are assumed; that is, if all conditions are the same, the same things will happen; and this dependability constitutes lawfulness, conformity to fundamental laws of nature. There are some who believe that this is not true of human behavior, which they regard as inherently unpredictable. If one assumes that behavior does not have any pattern, then it is a waste of time to try to investigate it scientifically. The alternative is to assume as a working hypothesis that behavior is lawful, and to see how far we may go in the application of scientific method to the understanding of behavior.

Planned, Controlled Observations. The ideal is illustrated by the following three essentials of the controlled experiment.

1) ISOLATION. All factors which would disturb the experiment must be either eliminated or compensated for. Sometimes one cannot eliminate an undesired factor, but he can make

allowances for its effects if he has measured these effects separately. Similar logic underlies the use in research of what is called a *control group* to assess the effects of all disturbing factors which cannot be eliminated from the experiment.

A control group is one which in every important way—except the condition to be investigated—is like the *experimental group* on whom the experiment is performed. For instance, one undesired factor in evaluating preventives for seasickness is that taking a pill can have a psychological effect on the takers as well as a medicinal effect. So, when a new preventive for seasickness is to be tried out on an experimental group of subjects, there must also be a control group of subjects who, without knowing that they are in a control group, are treated in every way like the experimental group except that they receive pills which, though appearing genuine, actually have no medicinal effect whatsoever. The effectiveness of the new medicine being tried out is then judged by how much more seasickness is prevented in the experimental group than in the control group.

2) VARIATION.   One factor is varied in order to discover whether it affects another, and, if so, how. For example, stimuli of one sort or another are varied in order to find out their effects. These stimuli are varied independently of an organism's response to them, and may be thought of as the antecedents of behavior. Those aspects of behavior that change due to stimuli being presented are responses. In any psychological experiment, out of all the possible stimuli that affect the organism, only one at a time can be varied if lawful response changes are to be attributed to it. All factors must be held constant during the experiment except for one stimulus. Some complicated experiments may appear to violate this rule, but on closer examination such experiments usually turn out to be composed of sub-experiments in which only one stimulus at a time is varied.

3) REPETITION.   A research finding is reliable only if it can be obtained repeatedly. Any competent investigator, anywhere, should be able to set up the same conditions and obtain the same result. If a given result is obtained only sometimes, then the conditions affecting it are not well enough known.

Other Methods in Psychology.   Even though the scientific method is most often thought of in terms of its applicability to laboratory experimentation, other research techniques are commonly employed in psychology that do not involve laboratory experiments but which still follow the principles of objectivity, lawfulness, and planned, controlled observation. As we have seen, many meaningful questions in psychology cannot be studied in the laboratory. We shall now note two techniques that employ the scientific method but are not used in laboratories.

Observation. To study some behavior meaningfully, one must observe it in its natural setting rather than contriving its appearance under closely controlled laboratory conditions. Studies of childhood and animal behavior, for instance, use this method. In this case, the experimenter does not manipulate or control the stimuli. Instead, he locates the source of stimuli meaningful to the organism, studies the characteristics of these stimuli, and notes the nature of the relationship between these stimuli and the responses they elicit. The experimenter must be certain that he can consistently and reliably recognize the relevant behavior, and he should also be able to train others to do the same. He must also find a way to record his observations as well as analyze them.

Clinical Methods. Clinical methods typically involve some combination of observation and an interview or battery of psychological tests. This method is particularly useful in the study of personality and personality disorders. Standardized observational and interview techniques are used in an attempt to ensure objectivity. Attempts are made to pinpoint the influence of developmental factors and/or situational factors on our personalities and our personality problems in day-to-day living. Clinical methods are also widely used in the assessment of learning and perceptual difficulties in children. As in other methodologies, the clinician attempts to isolate the factors that consistently lead to personality difficulties or learning and perceptual problems. He attempts to define the relationship between several of these factors and various different behavioral consequences. In order to strengthen the reliability of his hypothesis, he attempts to find many examples of the relationship that he is suggesting.

THE ETHICS INVOLVED IN PSYCHOLOGICAL RESEARCH AND THERAPY

Psychologists dealing with animals and humans have the obligation to behave ethically and considerately toward their subjects. The American Psychological Association has made policy statements concerning patient-therapist relationships, the proper use of psychological tests, and the conducting of experimental research on animals and humans.

Standards in Research on Animals. Research dealing with animals requires that the subjects be housed under certain standards of cleanliness and in cages of a sufficient size to allow freedom of movement. Adequate food, water, and ventilation must be provided. Experimental animals are not to endure unnecessarily painful experimental procedures. Should it be necessary to sacrifice an animal for experimental purposes, it is to be done as quickly and painlessly as possible.

Standards in Research on Humans. There are several ethical requirements which must be met before research involving humans can be undertaken. The experimenter must obtain the consent of the subject before the subject may participate in the study. Insofar as it is possible without compromising the aim of the experiment, the experimenter must describe the purpose of the study. Subjects are not to be told how they performed in comparison with other subjects, but are only to be given the general results of the whole group if they request them. Subjects are not to be forced to participate, and a subject's anonymity is to be protected.

THE DIVERSITY OF PSYCHOLOGY

In this book we have discussed a number of subdisciplines in psychology. These have included the following areas of psychological expertise: experimental, developmental, cognitive, industrial, personality, clinical, educational, and social. Specialists in these areas work in a variety of settings. Some of these include business, industry, government, colleges and universities, schools, community mental health centers, hospitals of various kinds, and private practice.

In reading this book you have seen how diversified contemporary psychology is. There are so many subdisciplines in psychology that we would be correct in saying that psychology is whatever psychologists do. The methods, problems, and rationale of different areas of psychology are very different. The type of training that psychologists receive also varies considerably. However, underlying this diversity are several common characteristics. All psychologists are interested in the accurate *description* of phenomena related to behavior in one way or another;

they are interested in the *lawfulness and regularity* in behavior; they are interested in the *prediction* of behavior; and they are interested in the *application* of basic psychological principles to problems in everyday living.

Appendix

Statistical Methods in Psychology

Definition and Procedure. Statistical methods are methods for making inferences about "populations," based on samples drawn from those populations. *Population* here refers to any group in which one is interested. One may want to know about all color-blind people, all Brazilian voters, all the radios produced in 1976, all atoms of gold, etc. Since it is impractical to study every member of such populations, one tries to obtain a sample which is reasonably representative of the population one is interested in, and to infer from the sample what the population is like.

Once the data have been obtained from the sample, two steps commonly follow. First, the sample data are summarized by means of a *descriptive statistic*; second, a *statistical inference* about the population is made.

DESCRIPTIVE STATISTICS

Correlation Coefficient. The coefficient of correlation is an index of the degree of relationship between two sets of paired measurements. For instance, the correlation coefficient could be used to show that hourly temperature readings on a Fahrenheit and a Celsius thermometer side by side were almost perfectly related to each other, or that the heights and weights of people are moderately related, taller people tending to weigh more than shorter people, though with exceptions.

Numerically, the correlation coefficient can have values ranging from +1.00 through zero to —1.00. A correlation coefficient of +1.00 indicates a perfect positive correlation, one of +0.60 indicates a moderate positive correlation, one of zero indicates no correlation, and one of —1.00 indicates a perfect negative correlation.

A positive correlation shows that larger numbers from one set of data tend to be associated with larger numbers in the other set. A negative correlation shows that larger numbers from one set of data tend to be associated with smaller numbers in the other set. For instance, you would expect I.Q. to be positively correlated with the number of correct answers in a course examination, but to be negatively correlated with the number of wrong answers. Thus, the sign of the correlation coefficient gives no information about the strength of a relation, but only about its direction. A correlation coefficient of +0.60 indicates the same strength of relationship as one of —0.60.

Do not be misled by the decimal expression of the correlation coefficient into thinking that it has anything to do with percentages. A correlation of 0.60 does not indicate that the paired data show 60% of the maximum possible relationship. For our purposes, it must suffice to say that a correlation of 0.40 indicates less relationship than one of 0.50 or —0.60, and that for those with experience in dealing with correlation coefficients, they provide very useful information. For example, when a college admissions officer is considering applicants' scores on an aptitude test, it is important for him to know the correlation coefficient between test scores and college grades, since this tells him to what degree he may expect to predict grades successfully from the test scores.

Measures of Central Tendency. A measure of central tendency indicates what numerical value the data tend to center around. The word *average* is an everyday term for this idea. Because there are several kinds of average, each has its own special name. The measures of central tendency commonly used in psychological work are the arithmetic mean, the median, and occasionally the mode.

Arithmetic Mean. This measure, often referred to simply as the mean, is what the layman usually means by "average." The arithmetic mean of a set of measurements is obtained by adding them all up, and then dividing by the number of measurements that were totaled. The arithmetic mean is often the most desirable measure to use, but does have the disadvantage of being considerably influenced by numbers which differ greatly from it. For instance, to offer an extreme example, suppose that in a small town there are nine men with an annual income of $100, and one man whose annual income is $200,000. It is mathematically correct to say that the mean income in this town is $20,090 per year, but the statement is rather misleading. An automobile dealer might think that there would be a good chance of selling 10 cars in a town of 10 men who had a mean annual income of $20,090, but upon arrival in town would learn that the arithmetic mean can be a poor indicator of most residents' financial condition.

The Median.   The median is the point which separates the data into an upper and lower half. For example, suppose there are five children whose ages are 6, 7, 9, 16, and 19. The median age of this group is 9 years. The number of children above this age is equal to the number of children below it. (The order in which the data are given will not affect the median.) If there is an even number of data, the median by definition must fall between two of them and the median is then defined as the mean of the two values it falls between. For instance, suppose that the 19-year-old left the group just referred to. The median age would then be somewhere between 7 and 9, thus dividing the group into an upper and lower half. The median age of the group would by definition be 8 years, the age halfway between 7 and 9, which is the arithmetic mean of these two values.

The median is used when the influence of extremely deviant values, or of missing values, is to be eliminated. In the group of five children described above, the median age would remain 9 years if the 19-year-old were to be replaced by somebody 109 years old, or if his age were unknown except for the fact that it was more than 9.

For reasons to be described below under "Statistical Inference," the arithmetic mean is used rather than the median unless there is some good reason not to, such as those just described.

The Mode.   The mode is the value which occurs most frequently in the group. For example, if there are more 9-year-olds in a group than there are children of any other single age, the modal age of the group is 9 years. Except to convey this particular kind of information, the mode sees little use in psychology.

Measures of Variability. A measure of central tendency tells only part of the story. Frequently, we also want to know whether the data cluster close to this statistic, or scatter widely about it. Three of the descriptive statistics which convey this information are the range, the semi-interquartile range, and the standard deviation.

The Range. The range is the difference between the highest and the lowest score. If the intelligence quotients of a room full of children range from 95 to 115, the range is 20. The range has the advantage of being easily understood, and the disadvantage of being based on only two cases, no matter how large the group, and therefore not being very reliable.

The Semi-Interquartile Range. This statistic is obtained by finding the range which includes the middle 50 per cent of the cases, and then dividing this range by 2. This is done by first finding the first and third quartiles, the first quartile being the point below which the lowest 25 per cent of the measurements fall, and the third quartile being the point above which the highest 25 per cent of the measurements fall. Therefore the middle 50 per cent of the cases fall between these two points, and subtracting the value of the first quartile from that of the third gives the interquartile range. This range divided by two is the semi-interquartile range. For example, suppose that the following eight measurements have been obtained:

75
64
62
51
48
33
30
15

To find the first quartile, find the point below which the lowest 25 per cent of the measurements fall. The first quartile is between 30 and 33. The same rule is followed here that is followed when the median falls between two measurements, and computing the arithmetic mean of the two measurements adjacent to the first quartile gives its value as 31.5. The same procedure for locating the third quartile gives its value as 63.0. The interquartile range, which is the difference between these two points, is 31.5. The semi-interquartile range is half of this, which is 15.75.

The semi-interquartile range, like the median, is not affected by extreme values, or by missing measurements if it is known on which side of the quartiles the measurements would be. For reasons to be described under "Statistical Inference," the semi-interquartile range is unlikely to be used as a measure of variability when the standard deviation can be used.

The Standard Deviation. This measure of variability is rather more complicated to calculate than the preceding two are, but it sees frequent use because of its importance in statistical inference.

First, one computes the arithmetic mean of the data. Second, one computes for each measurement the amount by which it deviates from the mean. Third, each of these deviations is squared. Fourth, the squared deviations are added together. Fifth, this total is divided by the number of items which were added. (In other words, steps 4 and 5 result in finding the arithmetic mean of the squared deviations.) Sixth, one extracts from the resulting number its square root. The result of these operations is the standard deviation, symbolized by the Greek lower-case letter sigma (σ). Here is an example:

Score	Deviation from mean	Deviation squared
7	+1	1
9	+3	9
3	−3	9
10	+4	16
2	−4	16
9	+3	9
5	−1	1
4	−2	4
3	−3	9
8	+2	4
TOTAL = 60		TOTAL = $\overline{78}$
MEAN = 6.0		

$$\frac{\text{Total}}{\text{No. of cases}} = \frac{10}{78} = 7.8$$

Standard Deviation = $\sqrt{7.8} = 2.79 = \sigma$

If measurements are on a random sample of a population, then to obtain an unbiased estimate of the population standard deviation we would have to divide by the number of cases minus one. In this example we would divide by 9 instead of 10.

The Normal Curve.   The normal curve is also called the *normal frequency distribution*, or the *Gaussian distribution*, after the German mathematician Karl Friedrich Gauss (1777–1855), who developed several essential statistical concepts. It is an important member of the family of frequency distributions.

Frequency Distributions.   A frequency distribution shows the frequency with which each measurement occurred in a group of measurements. That is, it shows how often each value occurred in the data. Frequency distributions are often presented as graphs, with the measured values along the abscissa (base line), and the number of occurrences of each value on the ordinate. For instance, the graph in Figure 19 shows that in a certain classroom there were five children who were 48 inches tall, and six children who were 51 inches tall.

The Normal Curve Defined.   The normal curve is a particular frequency function, illustrated in Figure 20. The mathematical equation describing this curve contains only three variables, the arithmetic mean of the distribution, the standard deviation of the distribution, and the number of measurements

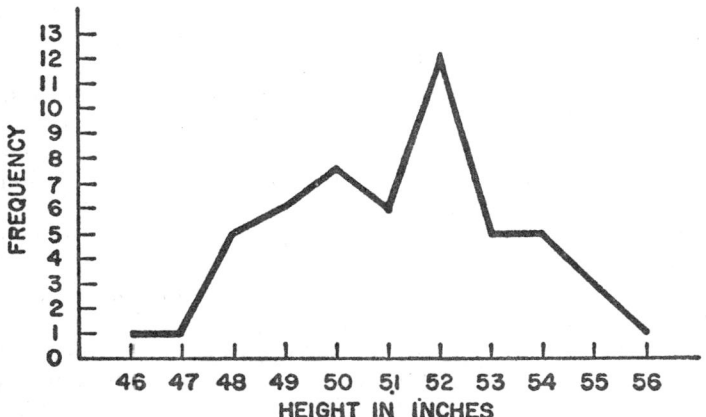

Fig. 19.   Frequency Distribution

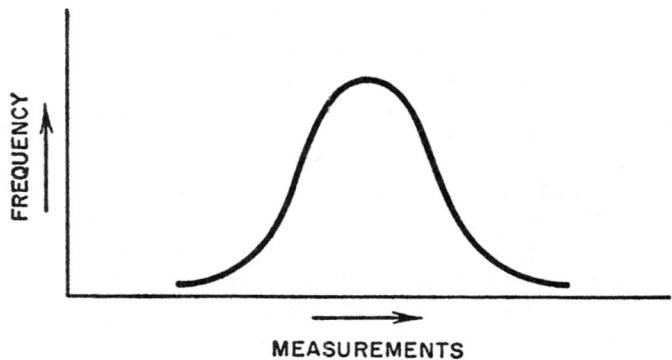

MEASUREMENTS

Fig. 20.   The Normal Curve

making up the frequency distribution. If one knows these three values for any normal distribution, he can then calculate how often any particular value occurs in that frequency distribution.

The most important use which is made of the normal distribution is in connection with problems of statistical inference.

STATISTICAL INFERENCE

Once the descriptive statistics have been computed for a sample, the next question is how representative these statistics are of the corresponding statistics for the entire population from which this sample was drawn. If the sample was drawn by random methods, one can calculate the probability that the sample statistic is within a certain range of the corresponding population statistic. This is because the sampling distributions for many statistics are known.

Sampling Distributions.   Suppose you repeatedly took samples of the same size from a large population, and for each sample computed the arithmetic mean. Suppose that after you had done this a thousand times, you prepared a graph of the frequency distribution of these thousand sample means. You would find that this frequency distribution was a very good approximation to the normal curve. This example illustrates that the sampling distribution of a statistic is the frequency distribution obtained for that statistic from repeated samples of the same population.

Very often, the sampling distribution for a statistic is the normal curve.

The Normal Curve and Statistical Inference. Here is an example showing how the normal curve is used in a problem of statistical inference. Suppose that a random sample of 400 school children in a certain state are given I.Q. tests. The mean of their I.Q.'s is 105, and the estimated standard deviation of the population I.Q.'s is 16. What can we infer from this sample about the mean I.Q. of all the children in the state?

We know that the sampling distribution of the mean is the normal curve, and a further fact is that the center of such a sampling distribution coincides with the population mean. It is clear from looking at the sampling distribution in Figure 21 that the majority of sample means will not differ too greatly from the population mean, and that it is relatively unlikely that a particular sample mean will differ so greatly from the population mean that it falls in one of the tails of the sampling distribution. The task is to make these statements quantitative.

Notice in Figure 21 the two little marks labeled plus and minus 1.96σ. In any normal distribution, 95 per cent of the cases occur between these two points. If we translate 1.96σ into the corresponding values of I.Q., then we will know the limits between which 95% of the means of samples like the one we have would fall. Then we will have a good idea of the prob-

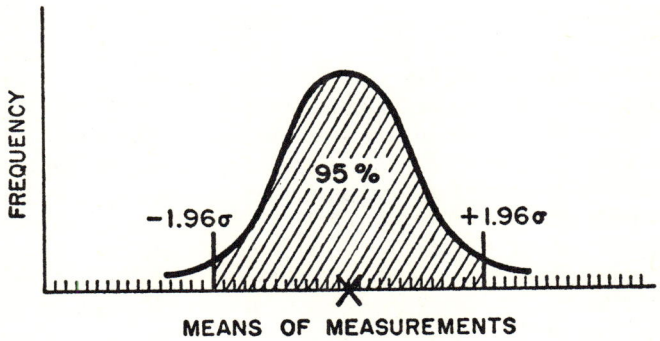

MEANS OF MEASUREMENTS

Fig. 21. Sampling Distribution. The point "X" on the scale of measurements indicates the value of the arithmetic mean of the population from which these samples were drawn.

able accuracy to be expected of samples of this size from this population.

First we must calculate an estimate of the standard deviation of the frequency distribution of sample means shown in Figure 21. (It has to be an estimate because we have only one sample mean.) This is done by first calculating the standard deviation of the scores in our sample as described on page 202, except that before dividing by the number of measurements, we first subtract one from that number. (In the I.Q. example, this means that we divide by 399 instead of 400. This provides an unbiased estimate of the standard deviation in the population.) The resulting estimate of the standard deviation of the population is now divided by the square root of the number of cases in the sample, and this gives us the Standard Error of the Mean. The Standard Error of the Mean is the technical name for the standard deviation of the frequency distribution of means, and this is what we need.

(Do not confuse the standard deviation of the population with the Standard Error of the Mean. Be sure to note that they refer to two different frequency distributions.)

Remember that the estimated standard deviation of the I.Q.'s in our population was 16. Dividing 16 by 20 (the square root of 400) gives 0.80 I.Q. points as the standard error of the mean.

To translate into I.Q.'s the two points in Figure 21 which are labeled plus and minus 1.96σ, we multiply 1.96 by 0.80 and get plus and minus 1.568 I.Q. points.

Remember that 95 per cent of sample means fall between these two points, and that the sampling distribution is centered on the population mean. Then it follows that 95 per cent of the means of samples of this size will not be more than 1.568 I.Q. points different from the population mean. Therefore we are reasonably sure that our particular sample mean of 105 is not more than 1.568 I.Q. points away from the population mean. Thus our statistical inference is that the mean I.Q. of the school children in the state is 105 plus or minus 1.568.

Of course we cannot be sure that our particular sample mean is not one of the 5 per cent which differ from the population mean by more than this. Statistical inference from samples cannot provide certainty. What it can provide is a calculation of the probability that an error does not exceed a given amount.

Other levels of probability can be calculated if one prefers. For instance, to have a 99 per cent chance of correctly stating the maximum error, the standard error of the mean must be multiplied by 2.58 instead of 1.96. Then one could say that the probability is 99 per cent that the mean I.Q. of all the school children in the state is 105 plus or minus 2.64. To have a greater chance of being right, one must allow for a larger error.

A frequent use of statistical inference in psychological research is in deciding whether some stimulus condition had a significant effect in an experiment. Suppose two groups of students are each given the same poem to memorize, one group using massed practice and the other employing distributed practice (see Chapter 4). Suppose further that the group using massed practice took eight more trials to learn the poem than were required by the group using distributed practice. Since the members of these two groups are only a sample of all those who learn, one must infer from this sample whether there would be this much difference between means, or even any difference at all, if the experiment were conducted on the entire population.

It happens that the sampling distribution of differences between means is also a normal curve. The details of the calculations would not be the same as in the I.Q. example just given, because the standard error of a difference between means is not calculated in exactly the same way that one calculates the standard error of a mean. With this exception, the logic and the procedures are the same when one calculates the probability that in the population the difference between means is within a certain range of the difference found in the sample.

Null Hypothesis.   An alternative method of deciding whether some stimulus condition has had a significant effect is to test the null hypothesis. One temporarily assumes that the stimulus condition has no effect, that is, that there is a null difference between the groups. Then one temporarily assumes that any difference between the two groups resulted merely from sampling fluctuations. One calculates, with the aid of the normal curve, the probability that sampling fluctuations could result in a difference as large as that he obtained between his sample group means if the null hypothesis were true. If under those conditions there would be only a 5 per cent chance or less of obtaining a difference in sample means as great as the one he obtained, he concludes that it is unlikely that sampling fluctuations were responsible for his results, rejects the null hypothesis, and therefore concludes that the stimulus condition would be found to have a genuine effect if it were tested in the entire population.

There are other techniques of statistical inference, some especially designed for use with small samples, for statistics whose sampling distribution is not the normal curve, and for experiments of more complicated design. They all result, however, in statements about the probability of error in making an inference from the sample to the population from which the sample was drawn.

Index

Cell body of neuron, 12
Central fissure, 17 fig., 19
Central nervous system, 13-14, 78. *See also* Brain; Spinal cord
Central tendency in statistics, 199-201
Cephalo-caudal, 11
Cerebellum, 17 fig., 20
Cerebral cortex, 17-20; and conditioning, 39; and drinking behavior, 59; and sexual behavior, 62; and emotional behavior, 70; and vision, 95
Chemical stimulation of brain, 15
Child: development studies, 7-11; and brain structure, 16; and concept formation, 114; and language, 119-20; and interest tests, 134; psychoanalytic theories of development, 143; socialization of, 170-72; and self-concept, 180
Child-rearing practices: and personality development, 143; and culture, 165; and social class, 170
Chimpanzees, 8-10, 74, 120. *See also* Monkeys
Choroid coat, 85 fig.
Chromosomes, 5
Ciliary muscle, 85 fig., 93
Class, social, 165, 167-70
Classical conditioning, 25. *See also* Respondent conditioning
Client-centered therapy, 160
Clinical psychology: defined, 185
Clock, biological, 61
Closure, 82, 83 fig.
Cochlea, 97 fig., 98, 100
Cochlear canal, 98 fig.
Cognition: and brain hemispheres, 21-22; defined, 72; and emotion, 72-73
Cognitive development: and concepts, 114; and language, 119-20
Cognitive maps, 38-39
Cognitive psychology, 191, 192; and motivation, 63; and thought, 115
Cold receptors, 101, 102
Color: receptors, 86; defined, 88-89; mixing, 89-90; zones, 90-91;

"blindness," 91-92; in dreams, 111
Common sense, limitations of, 192-93
Community psychology, 158-159
Compensation, as defense mechanism, 150
Compulsions, 152-53
Conduction deafness, 100
Concepts, 112-14, 115
Conditioned response, 25-27, 189. *See also* Conditioning; CR
Conditioned stimulus, 26. *See also* CS
Conditioning, 25-40; and fears, 73; in personality theory, 141; as therapy, 161. *See also* Behaviorism; Behavior modification; Conditioned response; Conditioned stimulus; Learning; Learning theory of personality; Operant conditioning; Reinforcement; Respondent conditioning
Cones of eye, 86, 87, 91
Confabulation, 47
Conflict, motivational, 146-49, 151, 152, 154, 167
Conformity: in groups, 175-76; and dissonance, 179; and evaluating others, 182
Contact comfort, 66-67
Control group: defined, 194
Controlled observation, 193-94, 195
Convergent thinking, 115
Conversion reaction, 153-54
Cornea, 85, 88
Corpus callosum, 20-22
Correlation coefficient, 198-99
Cortical blindness, 18
CR, 26, 27-28
Creativity, 22, 117-18
Crisis interveniton, 159
Cross-validation of tests, 131
CS, 26-29 *passim*, 32
Culture: and emotional expression, 71-72; and intelligence tests, 126; and mental retardation, 128; defined, 164; differences in, 164-65; and personal space, 176
Cupula, 106
Curiosity, 65